CHRISTIANS & DEMONS

Armed & Anchored
FOR SPIRITUAL WARFARE

DR. JERRY JOHNSTON

CHRISTIANS & DEMONS:
Armed & Anchored for Spiritual Warfare
Dr. Jerry Johnston

Published by Crossroads Christian Communications Inc.
1295 North Service Road
P.O. Box 5100
Burlington, ON L7R 4M2
crossroads.ca

Editor: Daina Doucet
ISBN: 896930-56-5
Printed in Canada

ALSO BY
DR. JERRY JOHSTON

CROSSROADS CHRISTIAN COMMUNICATIONS INC.

For more than 50 years, Crossroads has shared God's love through television and other media with people of all ages and at all stages of their spiritual journey. Founded in 1962 by David and Norma-Jean Mainse, the ministry has extended through the years to have a global impact. *100 Huntley Street*, the flagship television program of Crossroads, began on June 15, 1977, and is the longest running daily Christian television program in Canada. Crossroads provides relevant messages of faith and inspiration for millions of Canadians and people around the world and interacts with viewers via 24/7 Prayer Lines. Crossroads has also been a highly respected and effective humanitarian aid agency for more than 25 years, having responded in times of natural disaster worldwide, raising funds and partnering with on-site, non-government organizations for emergency relief and long-term rebuilding strategies.

Crossroads CEO Don Simmonds leads the exciting vision for the future through a dramatic expansion of Crossroads ministries with the effective increase of media programs and content, harnessing all media platforms. **Crossroads 360** is a multiple-channel, online media service, proclaiming Christian faith and values to four billion people connected globally online.

Crossroads Centre Prayer Lines, **1-866-273-4444**, are available 24/7 to minister to you and help you follow Jesus Christ (available in Canada and the United States). Visit our ministry website at **crossroads.ca.** Peruse our e**store** to obtain excellent resources to build your faith. Go to **crossroads360.com** for all of our online video resources and search by topic, guest, or date. Be sure to email us with your questions or prayer requests through our "CONNECT" button at **crossroads360.com.**

Your financial support is essential for Crossroads to continue its long tradition of faithfully proclaiming the Good News of Jesus Christ. Mail your tax-deductible contribution to: **Crossroads, P. O. Box 5100, Burlington, Ontario, Canada L7R 4M2** or in the **United States** at: **Crossroads USA, P. O. Box 486, Niagara Falls, New York 14302.** You can also give online at **crossroads.ca.**

When you are in the Burlington area, stop by for a visit at the Crossroads Centre for individual prayer or a tour of our studios: **Crossroads, 1295 North Service Road, Burlington, Ontario, Canada.**

We count it an honour to serve and strengthen you in your walk with God.

CONTENTS

ACKNOWLEDGEMENTS

Karl R. Popper wrote, "No book can ever be finished. While working on it we learn just enough to find it immature the moment we turn away from it." And, while Popper struggled with his knowledge of God, we do not struggle with the reality of demons and the dark world. Nevertheless, no book could contain teaching on the whole of the demonic realm.

Gary Gerard, thank you for your keen insight to equip God's people with resources to strengthen them on their spiritual journey.

Don Simmonds, CEO and Chairman of Crossroads, thank you for your heart for youth in your unceasing desire for them to know God's truth and freedom.

Ron and Ann Mainse, thank you for your careful analysis of the manuscript and your helpful suggestions.

David and Norma-Jean Mainse, two spiritual giants, thank you for your decades of Christian service that has led a multitude of people to spiritual freedom.

Daina Doucet, thank you for key input as you edited the manuscript and assisted me in telling God's truth about the demonic and the power of Jesus Christ.

Thank you to all the caring people serving at the Crossroads Prayer Centre **(1-866-273-4444)** who tirelessly share the love and forgiveness of Jesus Christ with the thousands who call.

DEDICATION

To my gifted son, Jeremiah Jay Johnston, who earned a Ph.D
and has become a gifted apologist teaching people
how to put on the armour of God.

INTRODUCTION

E ccentricity and denial have characterized much of contemporary teaching and preaching regarding the devil and demons, and their incognito work in our world today. It is odd that many pulpits across North America are silent as we simultaneously observe such dramatic societal, cultural, and moral changes.

Our school grounds have become battlegrounds as we witness numerous young people across the nation kill and wound. The deadliest shooting in United States history rocked Virginia Tech University in Blacksburg, Virginia, as Seung-Hui Cho killed 33 and left 20 wounded. He was a devotee and worshipper of Columbine shooters Eric Harris and Dylan Klebold, who he referred to as "martyrs" in his disturbing "Multi-media Manifesto" that he sent to NBC.

Cho was a Goth just like the Columbine killers and he had the same supreme, venomous hatred for Christians, rich kids, jocks, teachers, authority figures and "normal" people as they did.

Newtown, Connecticut, teenage killer Adam Lanza was also a Goth dressed in black the day he arrived at the school and began his shooting spree.

Jared Loughner, the gunman who shot Congresswoman Gabrielle Giffords, a Federal Judge, and a nine-year-old girl in Tucson was a United States military recruit obsessed with mind control. He mirrored the circumstances of many other mass shooters in history.

The violence in our culture has grown to a mind-numbing level. In addition, paranormal entertainment has become normal in our culture with a plethora of movies, TV shows, and books on vampires, demons, murder, exorcism, and witchcraft. Author Stephenie Meyer, a Mormon, the most popular vampire novelist since Anne Rice, took the theme to a whole new level by adding young romance, and sold more than 100 million copies of her *Twilight* series. She stated that the idea for *Twilight* came to her in a dream.

We have come a long way from the 1968 satanic movie *Rosemary's Baby* based on Ira Levin's diabolical novel. That movie was an enormous success and copycat films that followed are too numerous to name. How has all of this entertainment become normal?

Roman Polanski's psychological thriller showed Allison MacKenzie (Mia Farrow) pregnant with Satan's child looking at *Time* magazine's 1966 cover, "Is God Dead?" in the obstetrician's waiting lobby. The same year Anton LaVey founded the Church of Satan in San Francisco and boasted of his early affair with Marilyn Monroe and of the famous satanic members in his church: Jayne Mansfield, Sammy Davis Jr., and King Diamond. In 1969 La Vey released his book, *The Satanic Bible* (over one million copies have now sold). A satanic-panic seemed to grip the nation for two decades and then the attention faded.

Former spokeswoman, priestess and daughter Zeena LaVey Schreck was baptized by her parents into the Church of Satan at age three, and became pregnant at 13. She has subsequently called her father "lazy," "very confused," "experimenting with various gimmicks," a "con man," and "attracted a lot of psychopaths"[1A] and has renounced the Church of Satan.[2A] Zeena founded the Sethian Liberation Movement, that aims to help people resolve painful issues through meditation and spiritual guidance. Her father, Anton Szandor LaVey, born Howard Stanton Levey, died October 29, 1997.

I was interviewed with Zeena on *AM Los Angeles* on KABC TV a number of years ago. At that time she was defending the

Church of Satan. Unaware, she told the viewing audience that the night before she had attended my evangelistic event in LA. During the interview I reminded Zeena that her dad's book, *The Satanic Bible*, has played a crucial role in many teens dabbling in the occult throughout North America. I have prayed for her a number of times and wondered about the tragic reality of being born into the family of the leader of the Church of Satan.

CNN *Crossfire* with Pat Buchanan interviewed me opposite Paul Valentine, the leader of the Worldwide Church of Satanic Liberation in Connecticut. I was in CNN's Chicago bureau and Valentine in the studio in Washington DC. I found it quite strange that there again I was pointing to the numerous crimes and bizarre teenage behavior that had been indisputably attributed to young people's fascination with the occult.

My travels have also taken me to death row at the Oklahoma State Penitentiary in McAlester, Oklahoma, where I filmed with convicted teenage killer Sean Sellers on a cold December night. That weekend I had spoken to 6,000 young people at the Oklahoma Youth Evangelism Conference and warned them about dabbling in the occult. Sean was 16 on September 8, 1985, when he shot and killed Robert Bower, a convenience store clerk. He and a friend Richard Howard had decided that because this man had refused to sell them some beer, he was no longer of use in the world. Their satanically-inspired thoughts led them to a decision of such evil. Sean claimed Richard (who later testified against him) chose Robert as the victim, but that he, Sean, actually did the shooting. Together they disposed of the weapon.

On March 5, 1986, Sean killed his mother Vonda Bellofatto and his stepfather Lee Bellofatto while they slept in the bedroom of their Oklahoma City home. Sean tried to disguise his guilt by arranging the crime scene to look like the act of an intruder. I froze with shock to hear that on that fateful night after killing his parents he stood at the foot of their bed "laughing hysterically."

At his trial Sean claimed he was a practicing Satanist at the time of the murders and that demonic possession (by the demon "Ezurate") made him murder his victims. Sean indicated that for more than two years he had spent hours performing private rituals in his bedroom using his own blood to write notes to Satan. "Demons were the beings that would do things I wanted done," he wrote in his confession. They were the keys to the power Satanism promised.

Sean started drinking and popping pills and soon found like-minded friends. According to Sean they met to drink each other's blood. Sean told me Ezurate wanted something more: "Ezurate wants blood." In his demon-controlled state Sean took this as a command to kill his parents.

Ezurate's personality blended with Sean's. When he walked the halls of Putnam City High School and friends hollered, "Hey Sean," he would correct them, saying, "My name is not Sean. My name is Ezurate."

The jury didn't buy it, and Sean was found guilty of multiple homicides. With Mick Jagger's former wife Bianca protesting outside the prison, Sean was put to death by lethal injection on February 4, 1999, at age 29.

Sean Sellers was the 13th execution of murderers who were under 18 years of age at the time of the murder, and the first in 40 years for murder at the age of 16. Sellers was the first, and remains the only person executed in the United States for a crime committed under the age of 17 since the reinstatement of the death penalty in 1976. The United States Supreme Court ruling in *Roper vs. Simmons* (2005) later decided it was unconstitutional to execute a person for a crime committed under the age of 18.

Sean told me how he came to Christ after someone inserted a Bible into his cell. Initially he had a negative physical reaction, similar to a convulsion, when the Scriptures were placed in close proximity to him in confinement, but later, as he began to read the Bible, he claimed to have fallen on his knees and received Jesus as his Saviour. In documents, Sean claimed to have read *The Satanic Bible* "hundreds of times" between the ages of 15 and 16 when he committed the crimes, and in a "confession" letter written from prison he reflected on this period of his life: "I got very involved in Satanism. I truly thought it was an honest way to live, and the rituals of it would enable me to control my life."

Very candidly, the most sinister work of the demonic is not the overt expression of Satanists or those who worship the devil. C.S. Lewis, the former Oxford-atheist-turned-Christian, wrote of the "gentle slopes" recommended to lead people astray from God. In my opinion, this is the cleverest technique of demons. In *Screwtape Letters* we find a master demon instructing the junior level tempter, Wormwood:

"That, my dear Wormwood, is the whole sad truth. There is only one thing we can do. We must redouble our efforts. We must do everything we can to make sure that these humans do not believe in Jesus. And if they do believe then make them lukewarm and too busy with other things to be of any use to him. We have some reason to hope. Much of the media help us. And there is such a climate of pleasure-seeking and materialism that often the Christians aren't any different from anybody else. Many Christians are uncommitted. Some are hypocrites. And we have got many sincere people convinced they are so guilty that they have no hope. Others are bitter and have closed their ears to the message of the Resurrection. Others are just self-satisfied and only care about now. We have laid some very good groundwork intellectually. Many educated

people have been kept from considering both sides and are firmly convinced that there is no intellectual basis for believing in Jesus. They don't know what we know and we are not about to tell them. Many of these people are even convinced that we don't exist! That's very good! In closing, I will just say, 'Fight on, Wormwood. I fear we will lose in the end, but let us take as many of them with us as we can. Their willful, selfish part of them gives us much fertile ground to cultivate. We may have lost the war, but let's go out and win some battles for our father below.'"(3A)

Believers in Jesus Christ accept the divine authority of the Bible. In the New Testament we read about the devil and demons in 227 references—certainly enough not to ignore. The Scriptures do not inform us of everything about the devil and demons, but provide enough information to help us wage spiritual war successfully. And, there is no question we are in an unseen spiritual war that requires us to "put on the whole armour of God" *(Ephesians 6:11).*

We will learn in the following chapters how essential it is for us to know the battle in which we are engaged. Demons reveal their most intelligent, damaging work in psychological warfare against the believer. First, their desire is to keep Christians illiterate to biblical truth that will serve as an offensive weapon against their attack. Second, these enemies, as we will learn, target the mind to depress, discourage, and destroy a believer's heart for God and Christian maturity.

Psychological warfare has been utilized by various nations of the world in battle for thousands of years. Timothy Thomas reports, "China's history of psychological operations (warfare) goes back more than 4,000 years. [The] main objective was defeating the enemy without having to fight; the main essence of war as attacking the enemy's strategy; the main principle of war as contending for control of hearts, minds; and morale."[4A]

During World War II psychological warfare was used by the United States, British, and German militaries. Many strategies were employed, among them: direct phone calls to intimidate enemy commanding officers and their families, pamphlets containing propaganda, dual-purpose radio broadcasts that were designed to be popular, but included news material intended to weaken morale under a veneer of authenticity, and shock-and-awe military strategy.

In a spiritual sense, the same techniques are used by demons to weaken Christians and keep them from their full, fruitful, gifted potential in Jesus Christ. Consequently, we must be informed by Scripture and steer away from the eccentric—making a claim where the Bible does not; and denial—acting as if demonic activity is make believe.

So, let's take the journey together and realize, "God has not given us a spirit of fear, but of power and of love and of a sound mind" *(2 Timothy 1:7).*

CHAPTER 1

————+————

HOW DEMONS WORK IN OUR LIVES

When you read the newspaper or watch the news on television, do you ever wonder what is behind all the mayhem, violence, and tragedy in our world? We have never lived in an era quite like today. For example, prisons in the United States and Canada are overflowing with inmates. The Department of Corrections cannot build new ones fast enough to meet the demand. The problem has nearly reached epidemic proportions.

Another example is the area of sexuality. Much of the Western world has seen a total loss of restraint of sexual expression. Nothing is taboo or too extreme anymore. Dignity and modesty that once characterized the Western world's sexual expression has been obliterated.

When we turn to political situations of nations, we find great unrest and turmoil. It seems the world is at a boiling point in so many areas—politically, economically, socially, and even spiritually. In major cities and small towns of the United States and Canada, people are struggling with emotional problems and drug addictions.

Why is all of this happening?

If we look to secular theories for an answer, we will be sorely disappointed. When we turn to the Bible however, we find a very clear answer: there is a world of unseen spiritual forces at work. In this book we will examine the work of demons in our world generally, and in the lives of believers specifically. As our study unfolds, we will explore six topics:

- how demons work in our lives

- how demons work in our world: their history and future

- how to overcome demonic influences through prayer

- how to identify and eliminate demonic strongholds in our lives

- how God uses demons for His purposes

- whether or not a Christian can be demon possessed

As we study these six topics relating to Christians and demons, it is important to keep in mind two key verses:

- "Finally, my brethren, be strong in the Lord and in the power of His might. Put on the whole armour of God, that you may be able to stand against the wiles of the devil. For we do not wrestle against flesh and blood, but against principalities, against powers, against the rulers of the darkness of this age, against spiritual hosts of wickedness in the heavenly places" *(Ephesians 6:10–12).*

- "Lest Satan should take advantage of us; for we are not ignorant of his devices" *(2 Corinthians 2:11).*

These verses will serve as our anchors as we explore the tumultuous sea of the demonic world.

Now, let's focus on two strategies demons have used to disguise themselves and their work in our lives.

TWO DEMONIC DISGUISES

The first strategy used by demons is stealth. They hide

themselves through the silence of ministers and churches in general. Unlearned ministers strive to make sure there is a lack of teaching on demons. This strategy has been very effective in the educated world of North America. As a result, many people both inside and outside the Church deny their existence.

How can our churches be silent about something found 227 times in the New Testament? That's how many verses there are about Satan and his demons in the New Testament alone! Those passages are in the Bible for a purpose. They are not there to frighten or scare us; rather, they appear so we will not be ignorant of Satan's devices (see 2 Corinthians 2:11).

One of the great Christian scholars to write on the topic of demons was Merrill F. Unger. While at Dallas Theological Seminary, Dr. Unger did extensive research on demons and pioneered the formal study of demonology. A student of his, Chuck Swindoll, wrote this about Dr. Unger:

> *The Church of Jesus Christ lost a gallant warrior of the faith with the passing of Merrill F. Unger. It was my choice privilege to study Hebrew under this fine Semitic scholar during my years in seminary…. Of special interest to Dr. Unger throughout his ministry was the subject of demonism. [He said:] "Certainly there is no excuse for the Church to surrender its charismatic power to heal and deliver from satanic oppression. In the very measure that it does, it advertises its spiritual bankruptcy and makes itself a weak institution that no longer commands the respect of the spiritually needy masses. No wonder multitudes are seeking spiritual reality in Oriental religions, non-Christian faiths, and occult-oriented perversions of Christianity. Christian faith is so devitalized by apostasy and so contaminated with men's opinions and a defective presentation of Jesus Christ that it has become a hollow shell, powerless*

to affect men's lives."[1]

The second strategy demons use to disguise their work is an eccentric, unbiblical over-emphasis on demons that is inaccurate and mocked by unbelievers. This concept of demons and their work is foreign to Scripture.

I believe that Satan loves extremist presentations of his work because they cause non-believers to think the Church is ridiculous and bizarre. At the end of this book, you will find a *For Further Reading* section on demonology that is faithful to Scripture.

KEY ELEMENTS OF THE DEMONIC

Read carefully what the Gospel writer records in Matthew 22:12–30:

Then one was brought to Him who was demon-possessed, blind and mute; and He healed him, so that the blind and mute man both spoke and saw. And all the multitudes were amazed and said, "Could this be the Son of David?" Now when the Pharisees heard it they said, "This fellow does not cast out demons except by Beelzebub, the ruler of the demons." But Jesus knew their thoughts, and said to them: "Every kingdom divided against itself is brought to desolation, and every city or house divided against itself will not stand. If Satan casts out Satan, he is divided against himself. How then will his kingdom stand? And if I cast out demons by Beelzebub, by whom do your sons cast them out? Therefore they shall be your judges. But if I cast out demons by the Spirit of God, surely the kingdom of God has come upon you. Or how can one enter a strong man's house and plunder his goods, unless he first binds the strong man? And then he will plunder his house. He

*who is not with Me is against Me, and he who does not
gather with Me scatters abroad."*

In this passage, we find that a crowd had surrounded Jesus
while the scribes and the Pharisees stood on the outskirts.
They were not close enough to talk to Jesus, but were talking
amongst themselves. These men were arguing that the reason
Jesus could cast out demons was because he was the head of
all demons. The Pharisees did not say this to Jesus directly, but
because Jesus knew all things, He knew their hearts and what
was in their minds.

In the first century, there was a lot of explicit demonic activity.
We find record of this activity in the Jewish writings from that
period. *The Talmud* contains some of the most eccentric stories
about demonic activity ever recorded. Exorcists in the first
century could make money as a sort of traveling carnival show.
The traveling exorcists preyed on people who were hurting and
in need. When they got ill, many people in Jesus' day would see
an exorcist rather than a doctor.

We also see in this passage how Satan works in the family.
Notice Matthew 12:29, "Or how can one enter a strong man's
house and plunder his goods, unless he first binds the strong
man? And then he will plunder his house."

Satan's strategy for attacking the family is to immobilize the
father spiritually. When the husband and father in a family is
incapacitated spiritually, Satan has greater freedom to afflict
that family. When a man goes down spiritually, he is likely
to take his family with him. This is why men, husbands, and
fathers must stay strong in the Word of God.

In Matthew 22:12–30, we see four key elements concerning
demons. Let's look at them.

**1. The demon possessed man described here was
physically handicapped (see verse 22).** Dr. Michael
Green, Senior Research Fellow at Wycliffe Hall, Oxford, helps

us understand the term translated "demon possessed" in this passage and in many other passages in the New Testament. He writes:

> *The word used in the Gospels is generally* daimonizomai *(see verse 22). It means, "to be demonized," "be affected by demons." It does not allow us to adopt the common distinction, made in some circles, between those who are "oppressed" by the demonic and those who are "possessed." All are simply affected by that maligning power, wherever it is situated... these evil spirits are organized under Beelzebub (see verse 24). The name means "Lord of the house or dwelling." And it is one of the names of Satan in the Scriptures—a very significant one. He wants to be master of the house in people's lives.*[2]

2. The demonic healing and exorcism caused the crowd to be overwhelmed. The Greek word means "to displace," "to be knocked out of one's senses." It is likely the man healed by Jesus had been known by the crowd for years. The people were well aware of the wild behavior he had no doubt exhibited while under the influence of the demons that had afflicted him. The tense of the Greek verb also indicates their amazement was more than just temporary—it was continuous. They were continually amazed by what Jesus had done! John MacArthur notes:

> *As was often the case, this healing demonstrated in one act Jesus' dominion over both the spirit of demons and the physical world of disease. Outside of the Trinity, Satan is the most intelligent being in existence, and he certainly does not assign his forces to fight against each other and internally destroy his own program. And it is further true that Satan often disguises himself as an angel of light (see 2 Corinthians 11:14). In that*

role he may pretend to cast out a demon by restricting its power over the possessed person in order to give the impression of a cleansing. That sort of supposed exorcism has been common throughout the history of the church and is practiced today by various cults, false healers, and exorcists.[3]

3. Jesus endured the Pharisees' derogatory remarks. Their question in verse 23, "Could this be the Son of David?" carries a pejorative tone in the Greek language. It would be better translated, "This really couldn't be the Son of David, could it?"

Even though Jesus was out of earshot of these derogatory remarks, He knew their thoughts. The translated word "thought" is a beautiful word that refers to one's ideas and imagination. Jesus knew not only what they were thinking, but also the thought processes that led to their final thought and subsequent statement of it. This passage gives us great confidence that Jesus is supremely intelligent and wise.

Notice how Jesus responds when He knows what the religious leaders are saying about Him. Remember that Jewish leaders in general knew the history of their nation well. They knew what had happened to the kingdom after Solomon died: it was divided and eventually fell to Babylon and Assyria. Jesus used this as a vivid illustration to point out the fallacious logic behind their accusation that He had cast out demons by the power of Satan.

4. In His rebuttal Jesus taught profound lessons regarding demonism. First, He taught that Satan has an undivided kingdom. The term "kingdom" suggests order, rule, and authority. In other words, Satan's kingdom consists of a hierarchy of demons.

Second, Jesus taught that Satan destroys a family by attacking and binding the "strong man," thus gaining access to every person in the home. Dr. John R. Rice notes, "Eventually some of our sicknesses, probably much insanity, some nervous breakdowns, and sometimes excessive anger, and slavery to liquor and narcotics are caused by demon possession."[4]

THE HIERARCHY OF DEMONS

The apostle Paul wrote, "Finally, my brethren, be strong in the Lord and in the power of His might. Put on the whole armour of God, that you may be able to stand against the wiles of the devil. For we do not wrestle against flesh and blood, but against principalities, against powers, against the rulers of the darkness of this age, against spiritual hosts of wickedness in the heavenly places" *(Ephesians 6:10–12)*.

Interestingly, the Bible frequently uses images of war to depict the Christian life. Spiritually we are at war. The translated word "wrestle" in Ephesians 6:12 literally means "hand-to-hand combat." In Ephesians 6:12, Paul outlines four levels of demonic hierarchy.

1. The first level is "principalities." This is a special reference to political realms where demons work to influence earthly rulers, kings, presidents, parliaments, legislatures, judges, and everyone else connected with the governments of the world. We see examples of this in Daniel 10:

- "But the prince of the kingdom of Persia withstood me twenty-one days; and behold, Michael, one of the chief princes, came to help me, for I had been left alone there with the kings of Persia" *(Daniel 10:13)*.

- Then he said, "Do you know why I have come to you? And now I must return to fight with the prince of Persia; and when I have gone forth, indeed the prince of Greece will come" *(Daniel 10:20)*.

The person speaking in these verses is the archangel

Michael. He is not referring to the human leaders of Persia; he is an angel. A human being could not detain him. Rather, he is referring to the demonic forces that were controlling and influencing the human leadership of Persia. They are called territorial spirits. These spirits influence the governments of our world. That is why we must pray for our government and its leaders. They are uniquely exposed to demonic activity and influences.

Theodore Epp, founder of *Back to the Bible*, comments, "It proves beyond the shadow of a doubt that evil angels seek to influence world governments and wherever possible hinder God's plans.... There seems to be no question that all earthly governments (from the main government on down to the smallest segments) are attacked by these evil spirits. They seek to manipulate and influence men who are in office."[5] Therefore, we must pray for our leaders regularly and fervently.

2. The second level that Paul describes is "powers." This plural term represents a very large section of demons of great strength and force. These demons are probably more numerous and somewhat less independent and powerful than principalities. Demons in this category have a particular method of operation and an assignment to attack the personal feelings and thought-lives of Christians. These attacks are the fiery darts that Satan throws at us. This is how Satan can influence what we do because our thought-life inevitably shapes our actions.

3. The third level is "the rulers of the darkness of this age." These are demons that encourage superstition, occultism of every type and all false teaching. These demons are the real workhorses at the command level. They destroy people's lives by spreading spiritual darkness.

4. The fourth level of demonic forces is "spiritual hosts of wickedness in heavenly places." These are religious demons that intrude into the highest religious experiences. They operate as "angels of light" *(2 Corinthians 11:14)* that speak to people through ministers behind pulpits and professors in seminaries, subtly spreading false doctrine that enslaves men and women in religious unbelief. This explains how people can experience an incredible peace and contentment in cults and false religions; these groups are saturated with these kinds of demons.

There is no question that demons have supernatural power to influence our lives if we allow them to get a foothold. The purpose of this book is to make us aware of how demons work in our lives and in the world so we can avoid giving them that foothold.

DEFINITION FOR THE WORD "DEMON"

Before we move further into our study of demons and the demonic realm, let's pause for a moment and explore the definition of the word "demon." Our English word "demon" is derived from the Greek words *diamon* and *daimonion*. It is translated most often as "demon" or "evil spirit" (see Matthew 8:16; 17:18; Luke 10:17, 20). The *International Standard Bible Encyclopedia* notes that the word "seems originally to have had two closely related meanings: a deity, and a spirit, superhuman, but not supernatural."

"The second of these meanings involves a general reference to vaguely conceived personal beings akin to men and yet belonging to the unseen realm."[6] Merrill Unger writes, "As spiritual beings, demons are intelligent, vicious, unclean, with power to afflict men with physical hurt, and moral and spiritual contamination."[7]

While this may seem extreme, or even bizarre, we must remember that the New Testament writers continually affirm both that demons exist and that they are active in the world. James 2:19 confirms their existence unequivocally: "You believe that there is one God. You do well. Even the demons believe—and tremble!" Luke, the careful historian and physician, also affirms the reality of demons in the world: "Now in the synagogue there was a man who had a spirit of an unclean demon. And he cried out with a loud voice, saying, 'Let us alone! What have we to do with You, Jesus of Nazareth? Did You come to destroy us? I know who You are—the Holy One of God!'" *(Luke 4:33–34)*

Again, Luke carefully describes an exorcism: "And as he was still coming, the demon threw him down and convulsed him. Then Jesus rebuked the unclean spirit, healed the child, and gave him back to his father" *(Luke 9:42)*.

Matthew also affirms the existence and future judgment of demons where he records the words of Jesus: "Then He will also say to those on the left hand, 'Depart from Me, you cursed, into the everlasting fire prepared for the devil and his angels'" *(Matthew 25:41)*.

Moreover, Jesus, God incarnate, affirms their existence. Look at the following examples:

- He commanded his disciples to cast demons out (see Matthew 10:1)

- He cast demons out himself (see Matthew 15:22, 28)

- He repeatedly rebuked demons (see Mark 5:8)

- He had complete power over demons (see Matthew 12:29)

- He described clearly his conquest over demons and Satan (see Luke 10:17, 18).

If we take Scripture seriously, we have little choice but to believe that demons are real and active in our world.

THE INTELLIGENCE OF DEMONS

Now that we've affirmed the existence of demons, let us examine eight characteristics of their intelligence.

1. Every demon knows who Jesus Christ is. This is a great comfort to us as believers. If Christ is controlling our lives, then demons are aware of it. They know who God's children are: "Now there was a man in their synagogue with an unclean spirit. And he cried out, saying, 'Let us alone! What have we to do with You, Jesus of Nazareth? Did You come to destroy us? I know who You are—the Holy One of God!'" *(Mark 1:23–24)*

2. Every demon must bow to the authority of Jesus Christ. Look at Mark 5:6: "When he saw Jesus from afar, he ran and worshiped Him. And he cried out with a loud voice and said, 'What have I to do with You, Jesus, Son of the Most High God? I implore You by God that You do not torment me.'" Luke also records Jesus' authority over demons: "Jesus asked him, saying, 'What is your name?' And he said, 'Legion,' because many demons had entered him" *(Luke 8:30)*.

3. Every demon fears the inevitability of its final punishment. Notice what Luke 8:31 records: "And they begged Him that He would not command them to go out into the abyss." Matthew 8:29 reveals the same fear: "And suddenly they cried out, saying, 'What have we to do with You, Jesus, You Son of God? Have You come here to torment us before the time?'" These verses clearly attest that demons are cognizant of a future impending judgment and punishment.

4. Every demon obeys when cast out of a human body by Jesus. Instances of these occurrences are replete in the Gospels. For example, Matthew 8:16: "When evening had come, they brought to Him many who were demon-possessed. And He cast out the spirits with a word, and healed all who were sick."

5. Every demon knows which Christians/churches are effective and which are insincere. Notice carefully what the demon says in Acts 19:15: "And the evil spirit answered and said, 'Jesus I know, and Paul I know; but who are you?'"

Clearly, Paul was not part of the Godhead, but the demon knew who he was. The demon knew that Paul had surrendered himself to God and was being used by Him. Remember the context of the passage: the demon is speaking to pseudo-exorcists who were trying to imitate what Paul had done. However, the demon knew that they had no real power.

6. Every demon hides the truth of Jesus' deity and ability to redeem the lost. First John 4:1–3 warns us: "Beloved, do not believe every spirit, but test the spirits, whether they are of God; because many false prophets have gone out into the world. By this you know the Spirit of God: Every spirit that confesses that Jesus Christ has come in the flesh is of God, and every spirit that does not confess that Jesus Christ has come in the flesh is not of God. And this is the spirit of the Antichrist, which you have heard was coming, and is now already in the world."

7. Demons can and will discern between those who are sealed by God and those who are not: "They were commanded not to harm the grass of the earth, or any green thing, or any tree, but only those men who do not have the seal of God on their foreheads" *(Revelation 9:4).*

8. Demons obey the command of God to physically afflict those chosen because of disobedience. First Corinthians 5:5 states: "Deliver such a one to Satan for the destruction of the flesh that his spirit may be saved in the day of the Lord Jesus."

Paul also wrote in 1 Timothy 1:20, "...of whom are Hymenaeus and Alexander, whom I delivered to Satan that they may learn not to blaspheme."

THE MORALLY EVIL CHARACTERISTICS OF DEMONS

Four characteristics clearly mark demons as morally evil:

1. The word "unclean" is consistently applied to evil spirits (see Mark 1:27; 3:11; Luke 4:36; Acts 8:7; Revelation 16:13). Demons influence much of the sexual deviancy in our culture and in the world today. Purity is so difficult for us to maintain. However, in spite of the difficulties, we must keep our eyes and our hearts pure—always. When you are attracted to something unclean or impure, it is often the work of demons energizing that temptation.

2. People who are demon possessed or influenced become "instruments of unrighteousness." I believe many people in popular entertainment today are being used by Satan as instruments of unrighteousness. Romans 6:13 commands us: "And do not present your members as instruments of unrighteousness to sin, but present yourselves to God as being alive from the dead, and your members as instruments of righteousness to God."

3. Demons seek to influence pastors to compromise and teach their false doctrines. Paul wrote to Timothy, "Now the Spirit expressly says that in latter times some will depart from the faith, giving heed to deceiving spirits and doctrines of demons" *(1 Timothy 4:1)*. Peter also warns the Church of false teaching influenced by demons: "But there were also false prophets among the people, even as there will be false teachers among you, who will secretly bring in destructive heresies, even denying the Lord who bought them, and bring on themselves swift destruction" *(2 Peter 2:1)*.

4. Demons have amazing, perverted power over the human body. They can cause:

- blindness (see Matthew 9:22–33)

- insanity (see Luke 12:22)

- suicidal ideation (see Mark 9:22)

- personal harm (see Mark 9:18)

- super-human strength (see Mark 9:18)

Moreover, they can inflict people with associated demons. Read carefully Matthew 12:43–45:

> *When an unclean spirit goes out of a man, he goes through dry places, seeking rest, and finds none. Then he says, 'I will return to my house from which I came.' And when he comes, he finds it empty, swept, and put in order. Then he goes and takes with him seven other spirits more wicked than himself, and they enter and dwell there; and the last state of that man is worse than the first. So shall it also be with this wicked generation.*

This passage reveals that demons can recruit other demons to join them in afflicting a person.

HOW DEMONS HINDER YOU

How do demons work in our lives? We posed this question at the beginning of this chapter. There are at least three ways demons work in believers:

1. Demons always oppose the work of God and spiritual growth in us.

2. At appointed times, demons cause problems for us, yet only with divine permission. As we will see, God can and does use demons for His own good purposes. Remember Job 1:12 and 2:7:

- "And the LORD said to Satan, 'Behold, all that he has is in your power; only do not lay a hand on his person.' So Satan went out from the presence of the LORD" *(Job 1:12).*

- "So Satan went out from the presence of the LORD, and struck Job with painful boils from the sole of his foot to the crown of his head" *(Job 2:7).*

3. Demons attempt to get us to believe lies about our real spiritual condition. Remember, our final, ultimate defense against demons is to run as fast and as hard as we can to God. James 4:8 makes this very clear: "Draw near to God and He will draw near to you. Cleanse your hands, you sinners; and purify your hearts, you double-minded."

DISCUSSION QUESTIONS

1. What are the two key verses for this study? Why are they so important to keep in mind as we study demons? Take some time this week and memorize them.

2. Discuss with a group, or write out on a sheet of paper what you currently believe about Satan and demons, and how they work in the lives of believers. At the end of the book, compare your list to what you have learned.

3. What are two strategies demons use to disguise their work in the world? To which disguise are you more likely to fall prey: skepticism or eccentricity?

4. What did Dr. Green say about the term "demon possessed"? How does that affect your understanding of the categories of demon oppression and demon possession? Is it legitimate for us to make a distinction between the two?

5. Knowing that demons work to influence our political leaders, are you prompted to pray more diligently for them? Make a list of leaders you should pray for regularly. Consider sending them an email telling them you appreciate their service.

6. What does James tell us is our primary defense against Satan's attacks? What does it look like, in practical terms, to "draw near to God"?

CHAPTER 2

HOW DEMONS WORK IN OUR WORLD

THEIR HISTORY AND FUTURE

The key texts we will examine in this chapter are the following:

- "And the angels who did not keep their proper domain, but left their own abode, He has reserved in everlasting chains under darkness for the judgment of the great day" *(Jude 6)*.

- "For if God did not spare the angels who sinned, but cast them down to hell and delivered them into chains of darkness, to be reserved for judgment" *(2 Peter 2:4)*.

Whether we are willing to acknowledge it or not, the Bible, particularly the New Testament, addresses the topic of demons extensively. The discipline of demonology is the accurate study of what Scripture teaches about demons. At this point in our study, it is helpful to ask the "so what" question. Why should we be interested in studying demons? Most people today avoid the topic, and, likewise, most churches are also largely silent concerning demons and their role in Scripture, the lives of believers, and world events.

Despite the seemingly low-level priority assigned to the biblical teaching about demons, it is essential for Christians to have a basic knowledge about demonology. Why? Because we cannot be successful in our Christian lives until we know how to defeat Satan's plan to make us ineffective as believers.

If you survey your life as a believer, how often have you experienced victory—a life lived above sin and spiritual defeat? Unfortunately, most Christians live defeated lives. Most of us know nothing of what it really means to live victoriously in Jesus Christ. Most Christians never really attain a level of God-honouring prayer and personal worship. Why is this so? Because most Christians are largely or wholly ignorant of Satan's devices, schemes and methods. Most Christians have never been taught how to wage a successful battle against Satan and his demons.

As we survey world history we see that millions of people throughout the centuries have lived and died in the clutches of fear and superstition. False religions have blinded men with counterfeit peace and assurance. Behind all this, according to the Bible, is a sophisticated network of demons dispatched to deceive men and women.

Dr. Unger noted in his study of biblical demonology that demonology was highly respected during the first several centuries of the Church's existence. In fact, the earliest Church fathers faithfully proclaimed demonology the way the Church had experienced it during its formative years, and the way it is presented in the New Testament. For example, Lactantius in his work *Divine Institutes*, composed just 150 years after Christ's life, wrote of demons that they were "the inventors of astrology, and soothsaying, and divination, and those productions which are called oracles, and necromancy, and the art of magic, and whatever evil practices beside these men exercise, either openly or in secret."[8] Lactantius argued that demons invent false belief systems to lead men away from the truth of the Gospel.

Just like today, degeneration and denial crept into the ancient Church regarding the teaching and understanding of demons. From the Middle Ages until the Reformation much of the Church's teaching on demons was bizarre and eccentric. Even the great reformer, Martin Luther, who helped wake the Church from her spiritual slumber in the 1500s, never distanced himself from bizarre teachings that regularly attributed to demons morbid and exaggerated activity such as fires, accidents, and other mishaps of life. For example, today's Roman Catholic church practice of lighting candles during times of distress or disaster originated in the ancient superstition that fire keeps evil spirits away.

Earlier we touched on the fact that Satan and his demons always try to polarize Christians at one of two extremes: eccentricity or denial. But with biblical demonology largely ignored by churches and pastors today, Christians are left severely handicapped and unprepared for the spiritual battle they face every single day of their lives.

In the last 75 years, the world has seen ominous signs indicating that demonic activity is alive and well. Take, for instance, the rise of Adolf Hitler and his systematic slaughter of 6,000,000 Jews. Most scholarly works on Hitler's life speak of him as a demon possessed man.

We can also look at the spread of communism and the Russian purges in which millions of innocent people lost their lives. The rise of evil on a global scale is unprecedented. German theologian and author Paul Tillich noted that demonic forces are active in controlling modern history. A fellow German theologian, Reinhold Niebuhr, also devoted considerable attention in his writings to the matter of "demonized civilization."

Let's look at one example of how demons have worked in the world to blind people from the truth.

During the 1800s a group of thinkers who called themselves the Higher Critical School arose from liberal seminaries primarily in Germany. These liberal scholars questioned the history of the Bible. Using subjective literary methods of analysis that had no basis in ancient Near Eastern history or archeology, these scholars dissected the hard facts of Moses' writings. They based the analysis on the different names for God used in the various sections of the first five books of the Old Testament that have been traditionally ascribed Mosaic authorship. Based on their subjective literary bias, these liberal Bible scholars denounced both Mosaic authorship and any inclination that the books recorded actual historical events. In doing so, these scholars rejected and ignored the fact that these books, sometimes referred to as the Pentateuch, repeatedly claim Mosaic authorship!

Later, by applying the same questionable literary methods, the same higher critical scholars attacked other crucial New and Old Testament books. As a result they rendered the entire canon of Scripture a mass of unhistorical myths and nothing more than a collection of Jewish folklore. At a fundamental level, the scholars approached the text of Scripture with the presupposition that denied the possibility of the supernatural.

As young theologians from the United States and other parts of Europe studied under these higher critical scholars, their errant teachings influenced the Church at large. As a consequence the authority and integrity of the Bible were slowly eroded. In fact, by 1925 many of the major seminaries in America had fully adopted the higher critical methods and viewpoints of the German schools with the result that colleges and universities in the United States dismissed the Bible as historically unreliable and unfit for honest academic consideration.

In universities today Bible courses are generally taught by men who are biased against a normal, historical approach to the study of Scripture, and against the acceptance of the miraculous or supernatural. It is not uncommon for professors of biblical literature to be agnostics or even atheists. Therefore, what began in the higher critical schools of Germany has brought about an almost universal rejection amongst those in academia of the Bible as a historically reliable document.

We would be naïve to think that a trend like this happened by chance. Satan and his demons have been active in this rejection of God's Word in the academic community. Satan desires more than anything that the world would be "religious" while rejecting the truth of the Bible and the Gospel it proclaims.

Demons are working in our world, influencing opinion and creating false teaching. In 1667, John Milton wrote this in his literary masterpiece *Paradise Lost*: "Millions of spiritual creatures walk the earth unseen, both when we wake, and when we sleep."

This attack on the authority of the Bible through higher critical scholarship is just one of many examples we can use to examine how demons work in our world today. However, in light of all this, we must ask the questions, Where did demons come from? And, What does the future hold for them? We now turn our focus to these questions.

ORIGIN OF DEMONS

The consensus among a group of respected evangelical theologians like Lewis Sperry Chafer, John J. Owens, G. Campbell Morgan, Charles Hodge, A.H. Strong, and A.C. Gaebelein is that demons are evil spirits or wicked angels who fell with Satan in his rebellion against God (see Isaiah 14:12–15; Ezekiel 28:11–19).

Satan fell because God cast him out of heaven along with the angels who had followed him in his rebellion (see Luke 10:18; Revelation 12:7–9). Even though Satan was cast down to earth, not all the angels who had followed in the insurrection were cast down to the earth with him. Some of them, as we have seen in Jude 1:6 and 2 Peter 2:4, were doomed to Tartartus.

Not all conservative, evangelical scholars however, believe this theory to be correct. C. I. Scofield disagreed with this position. He wrote: "Nothing is clearly revealed [about the origins of demons]."

Another view perpetuated by G. H. Pember is that there was a pre-Adamic race thought to have existed on the original earth (see Genesis 1:1). The members of this race, Pember describes, were "men in the flesh" who were somehow involved in the rebellion against God, and who, in the ensuing catastrophe, suffered the loss of their material bodies becoming "disembodied spirits," otherwise known as demons. Pember writes:

The oft-recorded fact that demons are continually seizing upon the bodies of men to try to use them as their own is taken as confirmatory evidence that demons are disembodied spirits, and that their intense desire for re-embodiment indicates that the intolerable condition of being unclothed, for which they were not created, is so overpowering that they will even enter the bodies of swine (Luke 8:32).[9]

Merrill Unger comments on Pember's theory: "This theory rigidly distinguishes demons as disembodied spirits, from angels—bad as well as good. Angels, it is maintained, are not mere disembodied spirits, but are clothed with spiritual bodies, since the children of the first resurrection receive spiritual bodies (see 2 Corinthians 5:2,3), and are said to be 'like or equal to angels (see Luke 20:26; Luke 24:39; Philippians 3:21).'"[10] Clarence Larkin, who followed Pember's theory, saw in the conduct of the demonized, when the evil spirit had taken possession of his victim for the purpose of physical sensual gratification, a hint that the sin of sensuality was the "cause of the pre-Adamic earth."[11]

While Pember's theory is intriguing and seems to fit together nicely, it has one fatal flaw: the Bible says nothing about any human race before Adam (see Genesis 1:26–27). Unger rightly observes, "The only created intelligences revealed to have existed before the creation of man are angels."[12]

The Jewish understanding of demonology at the time of Christ had degenerated into a system of almost incredible and fanciful superstition, in sharp contrast to both the Old and New Testaments. Unger points out, "The almost unrestricted range of activity, and practically uncurbed power of demons over human beings in popular Semitic demonism, left little dignity to man's free will."[13]

As we continue exploring the question of demonic origins, read carefully one more time the two key verses we introduced above:

- "And the angels who did not keep their proper domain, but left their own abode, He has reserved in everlasting chains under darkness for the judgment of the great day" *(Jude 6)*.

- "For if God did not spare the angels who sinned, but cast them down to hell and delivered them into chains of darkness, to be reserved for judgment...." *(2 Peter 2:4)*.

Notice what John MacArthur writes about these two verses:

These angels, according to Jude 6, "did not keep their proper domain," i.e., they entered men who promiscuously cohabited with women. Apparently, this is reference to the fallen angels of Genesis 6 (sons of God): 1) before the flood (see v.5; Genesis 6:1–3) who left their normal states and lusted after women, 2) before the destruction of Sodom and Gomorrah (see Genesis 6:6; Genesis 19).

The phrase Peter uses in 2 Peter 2:4, "cast them down to hell," is borrowed from Greek mythology. The Greek word Tartarus described a place lower than Hades reserved for the most wicked human beings, gods, and demons. The Jews eventually adopted this term to describe the place where fallen angels were sent. In Jewish thought, the word was used to describe the lowest hell, the deepest pit—the most terrible place of torture and eternal suffering. Jesus, in spirit, entered that place when His body was in the grave and proclaimed triumph over the demons during the time between his death and resurrection.

The phase "chains of darkness" is also quite interesting. One author notes, "The demons feared going there and begged Jesus during his life on earth not to send them there (see Matthew 8:29; Luke 8:31)."

Not all demons, however, are bound in darkness. Some of them are "reserved for judgment. One author has noted that the idea of this phrase is that, "These permanently incarcerated demons are like prisoners awaiting final sentencing. Tartarus is only temporary in the sense that on the day of judgment the wicked angels confined there will be ultimately cast into the lake of fire."[14] Revelation 20:10 confirms this: "The devil, who deceived them, was cast into the lake of fire and brimstone where the beast and the false prophet are. And they will be tormented day and night forever and ever."

In order to fully understand the teaching presented in Jude and 2 Peter, we must examine the Old Testament passage on which they comment: "Now it came to pass, when men began to multiply on the face of the earth, and daughters were born to them, that the sons of God saw the daughters of men, that they were beautiful; and they took wives for themselves of all whom they chose" *(Genesis 6:1–2).*

The key term in this passage is "sons of God." It refers to a different group from either the men or their daughters. *The Nelson Study Bible* notes, "The phrase occurs elsewhere in the Bible and clearly means "angels." Job 1:6 presents Satan and his angels coming into the presence of the Lord for an audience with His Majesty. In this passage Satan's angels are called "the sons of God," with the suggestion that these angelic beings were once holy ones who served the Lord, but were now allied with the evil one.[15]

William Barclay, the renowned New Testament scholar, explains this interpretation of these passages. He writes, "In this line of thought the angels, attracted by the beauty of mortal women, left heaven to seduce them and so sinned.... Jude says that the angels left their own rank; that is to say, they aimed at an office which was not for them. [Jude] also says that they left their own proper habitation; that is to say, they came to earth to live with the daughters of men."[16] Barclay concludes with this thought: "All this seems strange to us; it moves in a world of thought and traditions from which we have moved away."[17]

This ancient theory of explaining Genesis 6:2 originated in the second century before Christ. It maintains that "the sons of God" were angels who had sex with mortal women, and produced monstrous children who were demons born of spirit and flesh. The apocryphal *Book of Enoch* promotes this biblical theory. MacArthur, who has been influenced by this theory, writes:

> *The sons of God, identified elsewhere almost exclusively as angels (see Job 1:6; 2:1; 38:7), saw and took wives of the human race. This produced an unnatural union, which violated the God-ordained order of human marriage and procreation (see Genesis 2:24). Some have argued that the sons of God were the sons of Seth who cohabited with the daughters of Cain; others suggest they were perhaps human kings wanting to build harems. But the passage puts a strong emphasis on the angels vs. human contrast. The New Testament places this account in sequence with other Genesis events and*

identifies it as involving fallen angels who in-dwelt men. Matthew 22:30 does not necessarily negate the possibility that angels are capable of procreation, but just that they do not marry. To procreate physically, they had to possess human, male bodies.[18]

Most rabbinical authors, including the historian Josephus, Martin Luther, Delitzsch, Plummer, Gaebelein, and MacArthur accept this theory.

On the other hand, Chrysostom, Keil, Lange, Jamieson, Fausset, Brown, Matthew Henry, C. I. Scofield and many others reject this theory and believe the "sons of God" were sons of Seth and "the daughters of men" were ungodly Canaanites who intermarried with them.

Pember and Larkin connect the angelic/human sexual union not to demons, but to "fallen angels" who are imprisoned in Tartarus because of their crime (see 2 Peter 2:4; Jude 1:6–7). Unger observes:

Again, if the 'sons of God' are simply pious Sethites who mixed with the Cainites, the prominent question is left unexplained as to why their progeny should have been 'giants,' mighty heroes who were of old, 'men of renown.' Delitzsch, who espouses the 'angel theory,' speaks of this passage as 'the fountain of heathen mythology with its legends.' Again if the intercourse between the 'sons of God' and the daughters of men' were merely marriage between the Sethites and the Cainites, it seems impossible to adequately explain certain New Testament passages, and the reason why some fallen angels are imprisoned and other are free to roam the heavenlies. Since they chose to leave their own realm and to break the bounds and God-ordained laws of two worlds, to work havoc and vicious confusion, God wiped out the results of their disorder with a flood, and dashed them down to the lowest dungeons (Tartarus) to deprive them forever of the opportunity of causing further derangement. The region of their imprisonment appears to be a more doleful and terrible place of confinement than Hades, and is clearly distinguished from Gehenna (see Revelation 19:20; 20:10).[19]

In summary, while there is much we do not know for certain about demons, their origins, and what role they played in the activities of Genesis 6, we do know that Satan rebelled against God and that one third of God's angels followed Satan in his rebellion. Since we do not know how many angels God created, we do not know how many demons exist today. However, from the passages in Revelation that describe the hundreds of thousands of angels that surround God's throne, it is fair to say that there are multitudes of demons in Satan's service.

THREE LOCATIONS OF DEMONS

Having briefly surveyed the origins of demons, let us take a look at where demons are now. Demons currently reside in three locations.

1. Demons reside on the Earth. Demons have existed before the Earth was made, formed, or filled. Consequently, they know it very well. They have been on the Earth watching. They have watched empires rise and fall. Actually, they have influenced the rise and the fall of those empires. Job 1:6 explains that demons roam the Earth: "Now there was a day when the sons of God came to present themselves before the LORD, and Satan also came among them. And the LORD said to Satan, 'From where do you come?' So Satan answered the LORD and said, 'From going to and fro on the earth, and from walking back and forth on it.'"

2. Demons reside in Tartarus. It's a prison-house for

demons who were involved in the wickedness of Genesis 6.

3. Demons reside in the abyss. The abyss is the temporary "jail" for demons who will afflict men horribly during the future Tribulation period foretold in Revelation. Notice what Luke recorded: "And they begged Him that He would not command them to go out into the abyss" *(Luke 8:31).*

Remember the context of Luke 8:31: Jesus was about to cast demons out of a man. The demons recognized Jesus and begged Him not to send them into the abyss before their time.

Revelation 9:1–2 also reveals key information about the abyss:

> *Then the fifth angel sounded: And I saw a star fallen from heaven to the earth. To him was given the key to the bottomless pit. And he opened the bottomless pit, and smoke arose out of the pit like the smoke of a great furnace. So the sun and the air were darkened because of the smoke of the pit.*

The Nelson Study Bible explains, "The bottomless pit is the jail for some demons (see Luke 8:31). It is also the place of origin of the beast (see Revelation 11:7; 17:8). Furthermore, it will be the place where Satan will be imprisoned during Christ's reign (see Revelation 20:2, 3)."[20]

As we look at these passages it becomes very clear that we are in a battle. Perhaps you never realized this before, however, do not let this be a cause of fear for you. Remember, Satan is mighty, but God is almighty! As His child, you ultimately have nothing to fear from Satan and his demonic forces. Jesus has conquered death, Satan, and hell. When we understand who we are in Jesus Christ, we realize that we have nothing to fear from Satan and his demons. Satan cannot touch you apart from the Father's permission, and we know that God works all things together for good to those who love Him and are called according to His purpose (see Romans 8:28). Therefore, we can rest assured that any demonic activity we encounter has been allowed by God for our good and that He is in control of it all.

THE FUTURE DOOM OF DEMONS

We have examined where demons originated. We have discovered where they are presently. Now let's investigate where the Bible says demons are headed.

First of all, we must note that Scripture assures us that demonic activity will increase as we approach Christ's second coming. We see the evidence in the world today with the massive tragedies, school shootings, and terrorist attacks. Second Timothy 3:13 informs, "But evil men and impostors will grow worse and worse, deceiving and being deceived."

Demonic spirits are at work in the hearts and minds of people who do not know Christ, mostly in a covert manner. Even though the vast majority of people, especially in contemporary North American culture, have no idea that demons are working in their lives, it is true nonetheless. Read what Ephesians 2:2 proclaims: "In which you once walked according to the course of this world, according to the prince of the power of the air, the spirit who now works in the sons of disobedience."

Additionally, 1 John 4:1 reminds us to be aware of the false teaching in the Church that is influenced by demons: "Beloved, do not believe every spirit, but test the spirits, whether they are of God; because many false prophets have gone out into the world."

During the Tribulation there will be an absolute invasion of demonic spirits in the seven-year period after Christ returns for His saints. Revelation 13:7 explains: "It was granted to him to make war with the saints and to overcome them. And authority was given him over every tribe, tongue, and nation. All who dwell on the earth will worship him, whose names have not been written in the Book of Life of the Lamb slain from the foundation of the world."

Demons work feverishly in our world today because they know there is an appointed time for their doom and punishment. This ought to serve as great encouragement to us. There will be a time when every demon, and even Satan himself, will be bound forever, never to torment the Earth and God's people again. Matthew 25:41 clearly teaches this: "Then He will also say to those on the left hand, 'Depart from Me, you cursed, into the everlasting fire prepared for the devil and his angels.'"

In Matthew 8:29b demons exclaim in the presence of Jesus, "What have we to do with You, Jesus, You Son of God? Have You come here to torment us before the time?"

It is clear from these verses that Satan's demons both know and fear their future destruction by Jesus Christ. Demons cry out, according to Mark 1:23: "Now there was a man in their synagogue with an unclean spirit. And he cried out, saying, 'Let us alone! What have we to do with You, Jesus of Nazareth? Did You come to destroy us? I know who You are—the Holy One of God!'"

Therefore, in light of all this teaching about demons, their origin, and their future, the most important question to ask yourself is, Am I in Christ? If you are, then you have nothing to fear from Satan and his demons. If you are not in Christ—that is, if you have not trusted in Him alone to save you from your sins, do not delay; do it today.

DISCUSSION QUESTIONS

1. Why is it so important that we study demons and learn to recognize their tactics in our lives and in churches? Why do you think so many churches have shied away from teaching about demons?

2. How did demons blind people to the truth of God's Word through higher criticism? Make a list of thought-provoking questions you would ask those who hold to a higher critical view of the Bible—ones that might cause them to question their presuppositions about the nature of the Bible.

3. How could you encourage a college student whose teachers reject the Bible and try to discredit the faith of their students?

4. Evaluate the different theories presented in this chapter concerning the interpretation of Genesis 6. Which position best accounts for all the biblical data? Taken in its context, what is the primary emphasis of Genesis 6?

5. Where are demons located today?

6. What is the final destination God has reserved for Satan and his demons?

CHAPTER 3

OVERCOMING DEMONIC INFLUENCES THROUGH PRAYER

I n the last chapter we explored the origin and future of demons. Although, we clearly observed that Satan and his demons will be defeated one day, we must also realize that they still have great power and influence in our world right now. Therefore, in this chapter we are going to spend some time discovering how to overcome demonic influences through prayer.

Keep in mind what Paul wrote to the Corinthian Church: "But I fear, lest somehow, as the serpent deceived Eve by his craftiness, so your minds may be corrupted from the simplicity that is in Christ" *(2 Corinthians 11:3)*. Remember that Paul was writing to believers. Therefore, this verse teaches that even Christians can be deceived by Satan and his demonic cohorts.

Additionally, Paul wrote to the Church at Thessalonica, "Therefore we wanted to come to you—even I, Paul, time and again—but Satan hindered us" *(1 Thessalonians 2:18)*. This passage vividly reveals that Satan can hinder and interfere with the lives and activities of believers. We therefore either have victory in this battle against Satan and his demons, or we are being defeated. There is no neutral territory or cease-fire agreement in spiritual battle. No third option. We are winning or losing.

The famous London minister, Charles Spurgeon, made this comment in reference to 1 Thessalonians 2:18:

> *This leads us to observe what wonderful importance is attached to the action of Christian ministers. Here was the Master of Evil, the Prince of the Power of the Air, intently watching the journeying of three humble men. And he was apparently far more concerned about their movements than about the actions of Nero or Tiberius. These despised heralds of mercy were his most dreaded foes. They preached the name that makes hell tremble. They declared that righteousness against which satanic hate always vents itself with its utmost power. With such malicious glance, the Archenemy watched their daily path. What cunning hand hindered them at all points!*[21]

Spurgeon highlights the fact that demonic forces are not as concerned with evil political leaders and nominal believers as they are with those humble Christians who have surrendered all to Jesus Christ and are following Him with their whole heart, soul, mind, and strength. When you and I live that kind of Christian life, we place ourselves in Satan's crosshairs for attack. He fears believers who are truly committed to Jesus, and demons will do anything they can to try and stop them.

THE BATTLEGROUND

We talk often about the spiritual battle in which we are engaged, but have we ever stopped to ask where that battle is being fought?

The spiritual battle is fought, won, and lost on the battlefield of the mind.

The brain is an amazingly complex marvel of God's creation.

It weighs only three pounds, yet it contains billions of cells that are capable of performing an incredibly enormous workload. Our minds are constantly generating, receiving, recording, and transmitting information.

Scientists have estimated that after 70 years of activity, a brain may contain nearly 15 trillion separate pieces of information. Thousands upon thousands of separate thoughts can pass through it every day, but the brain never gets tired. It is a magnificent thinking machine with a marvelous capacity. The sad reality however, is that many people do not use their minds and brains the way God intended. Spiritually speaking, they never use their brain to its full potential. Most of us seldom even use more than ten percent of the brain's capacity.

The primary target of demonic forces is the mind of the believer. The fastest and surest way demons can defeat a Christian is by attacking the mind. Demons attempt to infiltrate the mind with a host of anti-faith, anti-Christian, sensual lies aimed at bringing us to destruction. These evil and perverse thoughts are being hurled at us everyday and they are the firey darts Paul refers to in Ephesians 6. Proverbs 23:7 pronounces unequivocally, "For as [a man] thinks in his heart, so is he."

When a believer's mind is infiltrated by demonic suggestion, their prayer life is fruitless. Part of the purpose of this study is to understand where we are on the battlefield. How has your prayer life been lately? Have you been praying? Have you seen answers to prayer? For which lost person have you prayed whom you have seen come to faith? What new areas of obedience can you point to in your experiences that are the direct result of prayer?

Our victories over the enemy are not won in public. They are won in the prayer closet. A minister or Christian who does not pray is powerless. We have too many planning meetings and not enough prayer meetings. We have too many strategy meetings and not enough prayer meetings. We are far too inclined to talk about problems and never pray about them. This is why the Church often seems so powerless against the forces of evil.

When men and women of God pray as though prayer were their very breath, then and only then will the Church have the power to change the world for the glory Jesus Christ!

Before our behavior toward prayer can be transformed however, our thinking must change. The only way to change our actions is to change our thinking. This is why the mind is so relentlessly attacked by Satan and his demons. If they can cripple our thinking, they can cripple the rest of our lives.

Has your mind been warped by demonic influence? What kinds of thoughts do you have most often? Men, are you struggling with impure thoughts, pornography, or extramarital affairs? Young singles, are you struggling with personal purity? What kind of mind do you have? When you are at work, what thoughts cross your mind? When you are driving alone, what things are you thinking about? As you fall asleep at night, what is on your mind? What thoughts really fill your mind?

Scripture warns us about various minds, or thought patterns, and their spiritual defects. Let's look at four types of minds that leave us open to satanic attack and defeat.

1. A mind that is darkened. Sometimes our English translations render the word "mind" as "understanding;" however, the word in the original language also translates as the word that means "mind." This word (understanding/mind) refers to a person whose mind is fixed on futile, transitory things without eternal value. Paul writes to the Ephesians, "This I say, therefore, and testify in the Lord, that you should no longer walk as the rest of the Gentiles walk, in the futility of their mind" *(Ephesians 4:7).*

Again Paul writes to the Corinthians about unbelievers, "...whose minds the god of this age has blinded, who do not believe, lest the light of the Gospel of the glory of Christ, who is the image of God, should shine on them" *(2 Corinthians 4:4)*. Darkened minds do and say darkened things. Aleister Crowley, who provided inspiration for Anton LaVey (Church of Satan), represents a darkened mind. Known as the "Great Beast 666," he both explored and defined the dark world of the occult.[22]

2. A mind that is defiled. Originally the word translated "defiled" meant "to dye with another colour," however, it also refers to staining, soiling, polluting, or contaminating.

These believers' pretentious manner of living exposes the phoniness of their words. They claim to know God, but their lifestyles and minds are defiled, revealing the true condition of their hearts. Paul writes, "To the pure all things are pure, but to those who are defiled and unbelieving nothing is pure; but even their mind and conscience are defiled. They profess to know God, but in works they deny Him, being abominable, disobedient, and disqualified for every good work" *(Titus 1:15-16)*.

Our minds can be defiled by many things, but one of the most seditious attacks on our minds is pornography. Pornography stains the mind of a Christian. It neutralizes our passion for Jesus, undermines our joy in worship, and destroys our commitment to give of ourselves and our resources for Christ's work.

Focus on the Family's pastoral help line reveals that one out of seven calls are from pastors involved in internet pornography. Also, 35 percent of their calls deal with sexual issues that include the use of pornography.

3. A mind that is depraved. The word translated "depraved" means corrupted, destroyed, ruined, or spoiled. Paul writes, "Useless wranglings of men of corrupt minds and destitute of the truth, who suppose that godliness is a means of gain. From such withdraw yourself" *(1 Timothy 6:5)*. So many of the TV shows and movies produced around the world today reflect this mindset.

4. A mind that is dead. A "dead" mind is set on the flesh. It is the natural mind with which we were born, and includes all of our sinful inclinations. The believer is supposed to have a completely different mindset. Paul instructs us in Romans 8:6, "For to be carnally minded is death, but to be spiritually minded is life and peace. Because the carnal mind is enmity against God; for it is not subject to the law of God, nor indeed can be."

THE ENEMY OF YOUR MIND

When a person becomes a believer in Jesus Christ, God gives his mind new capacities—the ability to receive biblical and spiritual truth. The mind however, remains an active battleground.

Paul affirms this in Romans 7:23, "But I see another law in my members, warring against the law of my mind, and bringing me into captivity to the law of sin which is in my members."

Demons use mental schemes or methods to deceive the minds of Christians. In Ephesians 6:11, Paul commands believers to "Put on the whole armour of God, that you may be able to stand against the wiles of the devil." The word "wiles" is translated from the Greek word *methodius*. From it we get our English word "method." We must be on guard against Satan's methods of deception. Again Paul warns, "Lest Satan should take advantage of us; for we are not ignorant of his devices" (*2 Corinthians 2:11*).

Demons try to masquerade lies as the truth and infiltrate the believer's mind in an attempt to sabotage his or her faith. They are constantly working to create false doctrine and error.

The media is an incredibly powerful tool used by demons to implant false ideas and sensuality into the mind of the believer. Does this mean we ought to throw out our TVs and never go to movies? No, but it does mean we need to be discerning about what we put into our minds. Notice what 1 Timothy 4:1 says: "Now the Spirit expressly says that in latter times some will depart from the faith, giving heed to deceiving spirits and doctrines of demons."

PROTECTING YOUR MIND

God does not leave us unprotected in this battle for our minds. He has given us at least five means of protection and defense against Satan's attacks. Let's look at them.

1. The helmet of salvation. How do we protect our minds? By heeding Paul's instruction: "...take the helmet of salvation" *(Ephesians 6:7)*. Thus if someone is not a believer in Christ, they don't even have a chance in this mental battle. If you are believer however, you can claim and obey James 4:7: "Therefore submit to God. Resist the devil and he will flee from you."

2. Be filled with the Spirit. This is not just an option; it's a command. Ephesians 5:18 says, "And do not be drunk with wine, in which is dissipation; but be filled with the Spirit."

Christians are either in the flesh or in the Spirit. As you read this book, you are either controlled by the Holy Spirit, or by your flesh.

Have you ever gotten in a fight with your spouse on your way to church? I have. How in the world could something like that happen on the way to church? Because the devil wants to rob us of our peace. He wants us in the flesh instead of in the spirit before we worship God.

3. Allow the Holy Spirit to lead you to God's truth. Jesus said, "...when He, the Spirit of truth, has come, He will guide you into all truth; for He will not speak on His own authority, but whatever He hears He will speak; and He will tell you things to come" *(John 16:13)*. Why? Because when we know the truth, the truth will set us free. Unless we have truth, we will never have freedom.

4. Fill our minds daily with the Word of God. What does the rest of Ephesians 6:17 say? "And take the helmet of salvation, and the sword of the Spirit, which is the Word of God." The word Paul uses for "sword" in this passage is a specific Greek word which means "short sword."

Roman soldiers carried a short sword that could be pulled out and wielded quickly and precisely. Therefore, when I am struck with Satan's attacks—thoughts that bombard my mind—I know there is a passage of Scripture that addresses the issue with which I am struggling. When we fail to read and memorize the Word of God, our swords become dull and ineffective.

5. A concerted effort of total obedience to Jesus Christ. When there is disobedience in our lives, we open the door to demonic influence. Notice 2 Corinthians 10:5 says, "Casting down arguments and every high thing that exalts itself against the knowledge of God, bringing every thought into captivity to the obedience of Christ."

We must strive to bring every thought under the control of Jesus Christ. The word "obedience" that Paul uses in this passage means "to hear under." As captives to Christ who are "under" His authority, we need to hear every thought from our position of submission to Him. When we are faced with the temptation to sin, we must say: I am a captive of Jesus Christ. I cannot respond to that. I am committed to obeying Him.

THE MIND GOD DESIRES FOR US

What is the mind that God desires you and me to have? Look at Philippians 4:8: "Finally, brethren, whatever things are true, whatever things are noble, whatever things are just, whatever things are pure, whatever things are lovely, whatever things are of good report, if there is any virtue and if there is anything praiseworthy—meditate on these things."

This verse provides us with a filter by which to judge every thought that crosses our minds. Paul gives us a specific list of things with which we should fill our minds—things we should "dwell on," or "meditate on." The Greek word means to consider, ponder, reflect, to mull over, and meditate on. The tense of the verb in Greek indicates that the action is to be continuous. Let us examine each one of these eight "filters."

1. Think on what is true. Truth, in this case, does not only refer to what is not false, but to what is true in the sense of being real or genuine. Lies and gossip can only destroy us.

A Christian should obviously refuse to dwell on things he knows to be false!

2. Think on what is noble or honest. The word "noble" refers to things worthy of honour or respect. A healthy, Christian mind is not always occupied with foolishness and nonsense. It is a mind that has seriousness of purpose and self-respect in conduct.

3. Think on what is right or just. "Right" or "just" means to think upright thoughts and conform our minds to the principles of God's Word. It refers to the right way of looking at things from God's perspective. Every day demons seek to feed false philosophy into our minds through the media, unbelieving friends, relatives, teachers, and carnal Christians. But God wants us to develop the habit of asking whether or not something is consistent with His Word.

4. Think on what is pure. The word "pure" refers to moral purity—the absence of anything that stains, defiles, contaminates, or corrupts, particularly in sexual matters.

5. Think on what is lovely. "Lovely" refers to what is attractive, pleasing, winsome, amiable, or agreeable. It represents the pleasantness and graciousness that foster peace and harmony. We must forgive each other in order to enjoy these virtues.

6. Think on what is of good report. "Good report" means "to speak well of." In other words, we are to think good things about people—the things that speak well of them. Gossip is the opposite of "a good report."

7. Think on what is virtuous or excellent. The Greek word for "excellence" used in this passage only occurs four times in the New Testament. It refers to that which rises above the mundane, transitory, hollow things of this world, to that which is of moral excellence.

8. Think on what is praiseworthy. In other words, we are to think on things that have God's approval.

THE PEACEFUL MIND

Troubled minds are the great plague of our day. Nearly one out of ten Americans seek professional help because of emotional distress. Some doctors estimate that more than 75 percent of their patients suffer from symptoms that are induced by stress. Stress can make you ill and even kill you. But we do not have to live this way.

Take to heart what Paul wrote to the Philippian Church: "Be anxious for nothing, but in everything by prayer and supplication, with thanksgiving, let your requests be made known to God; and the peace of God, which surpasses all understanding, will guard your hearts and minds through Christ Jesus..." *(Philippians 4:6–7).*

Notice this is a command, not a suggestion! We are commanded to be anxious for nothing. The word translated "anxious" means "to draw in different directions," or "to be of a divided mind." It pictures harassing, distressing, distracting thoughts that keep us tense, unsettled, and confused. This is the same word that Jesus used in Martha's house when he said, "Martha, Martha, you are worried and troubled about many things." She was inwardly disturbed and agitated. This is the kind of emotion that ties our stomach in knots, puts deep wrinkles on our brows, raises our blood pressure, and makes us irritable and hard to get along with. Anxiety can paralyze us and even cripple our ministry.

What is the solution to this problem? Take everything to God in prayer. The word for prayer that Paul uses in this verse is a special word that refers exclusively to our relationship with God. It is a general word for prayer that doesn't emphasize our petitions or requests, but focuses on our communion and conversation with God.

God wants us to be conscious of His presence at all times. This means to be in constant communication with Him. He wants us to be aware that He is with us and in control of every situation. In short, He wants our minds fixed on Him! Isaiah wrote, "You will keep him in perfect peace, whose mind is stayed on You, because he trusts in You" *(Isaiah 26:3).*

Next, if we want to get rid of worry, we need to bring our supplications before God. The word "supplication" refers to a specific request for a specific need. We need to ask God to do explicit things that we believe He wants to do in our lives. We need to ask God for every need that is in front of us. How do you know if you are praying like that? Look at what the result is: "and the peace of God, which surpasses all understanding, will guard your hearts and minds through Christ Jesus" *(Philippians 4:7).*

The term translated "guard" is a military word that meant "to keep watch, to guard, or garrison." The concept of peace that passes all understanding implies a peace that will "blow your mind"! When God's peace is guarding our minds, it is more than the mind itself can conceive. It is beyond human comprehension, surpassing our wildest dreams. It is a supernatural peace.

If we want to have victory over the demonic forces that affect us, we need to be in constant communication with God, bring our requests before Him, and allow His peace to guard our minds in the spiritual battlefield.

DISCUSSION QUESTIONS

1. What is the primary battleground where spiritual warfare takes place? Why is this battlefield so important to both God and Satan in the life of a believer or non-believer?

2. We mentioned that in order to change our behavior we must first change our minds. How do we change our minds and thinking? Make a list of practical steps that can help one change his or her mind. Are you practicing these steps in your life?

3. What are the four negative states of mind described in Scripture that leave us open to demonic attack and influence?

4. Why are pornography and other sexual sins such powerful forces that draw us away from God and into a place of great spiritual vulnerability?

5. How does Philippians 4:8 work as a filter for our minds? Have you memorized this verse? If not, take time this week to do so.

6. What is the key to having a mind that is free from worry and anxiety? Take a moment to think carefully through the last time you were very worried. When should you have turned to God to avoid that worry? Have you confessed these sins of worry?

CHAPTER 4

CAN A CHRISTIAN BE DEMON POSSESSED?

I n this chapter we will explore an oft-debated question in the Christian community: Can a Christian be demon possessed? In seeking to shed light on this important question, we will cover five areas:

- define biblically what demon possession means in the New Testament

- examine how disobedience opens the door to demonic oppression in our lives

- discover through which specific doors Satan tries to enter our lives

- learn how to detect demonization in our lives

- uncover the keys for destroying any demonic activity in our lives

DEMON POSSESSION AND INFLUENCE

As we begin, it's essential to point out that in spite of our Western, rationalistic, anti-supernatural mindset, demonization is a reality. Our world today is filled with highly educated people who reject the supernatural and call demons a product of Christian eccentricity and anachronism. Yet both the New Testament and current events demonstrate the reality that demons exist and exert control over human beings. John Nevius, in his book *Demon Possession and Allied Themes*, recounts numerous instances of demon possession that he and his co-workers encountered in China during the last half of the 19th century. He wrote, "Demons often spoke to the missionaries as they were about to cast them out of a hapless victim. Some of the demons pleaded for mercy and resisted. However, they were always forced to leave whenever Christians prayed together and gave the command in the name of the Lord Jesus Christ."[23]

Archeologists have found manuscripts that record incantations and magical formulas for the expulsion of demons. Today in Southeast Asia and Africa pagan religious leaders regularly perform rituals to cast out evil spirits. The record of history establishes without any doubt that demon possession was a reality even before Jesus' coming to Earth. Moreover, the testimony of witnesses undeniably establishes that demonic activity has continued from the time of Christ until now.

Scott Peck, a psychiatrist, caught the public's eye with his book *The People of the Lie*. Peck challenges the traditional scientific approach that excludes evil and the supernatural. He writes:

> *The concept of evil has been central to religious thought for a millennium, and yet, it is virtually absent from our science of psychology, which one might think would be vitally concerned with the matter. The very word evil requires a value judgment. Hence, it is not even permissible before a strictly value free science to deal with the subject. There are many compelling reasons today for the reintegration of science and religion. The point: the creation of a science that is no longer value free.*[24]

Every person in the world, including you and me, has been directly or indirectly affected by demonic activity. Consider, for instance, this truth: we know that all men are sinners according to Romans 3:11, 23. We also know that all unbelieving sinners are controlled by Satan, the prince of the power of the air. These are the same men and women with whom we work and who live with us in this fallen world.

We live surrounded by a satanic world system in which demonically influenced individuals have had a tremendous impact on many lives. Take Saddam Hussein, for example. He killed and tortured hundreds of thousands of people. There is no question this man was influenced by demonic forces. Hussein is just one example of the many tyrants who have terrorized the world throughout history—a list that spans from Nero to Hitler. All of these people were influenced by demons.

None of us can escape the influence of demons because the world we live in has been so profoundly influenced by them. Eleven times in the book of Acts Luke records confrontation between demons and the members of the early Church. The first Church was constantly interacting with demonic spirits in their efforts to win men and women to Jesus Christ. How different our churches today are from the early Church! The average church today teaches nearly nothing about demons or Satan, yet Luke, guided by the Holy Spirit, considered it a significant enough topic to deal with it 11 times in a 28-chapter book.

Sixteen passages in the New Testament deal specifically with Satan's work in the lives of believers:

- Demons oppose the Gospel that Christians are commanded to spread and prevent people from understanding the Gospel (see Luke 8:12).

- Demons work feverishly to hinder Christian workers from proclaiming the Good News and wage direct warfare against believers (see Ephesians 6:10–12).

- Satan slanders believers before God (see Revelation 12:10).

- Demons plant doubts about God's truth in people's hearts and minds (see Genesis 3:1).

- Demons promote rebellion and stir hearts against what God is doing (see Ephesians 2:1-3).

- Demons tempt and prod people toward sexual sin (see 1 Corinthians 5).

- Demons try to distract our attention from what is eternal by drawing us toward the temporal and worldly (see 1 John 2:15).

- Demons try to compel men and women to depend on human wisdom and strength rather than on God's truth and might (see 1 Chronicles 21:1–8).

- Demons tempt us to be filled with pride when we have spiritual success and victory (see Ezekiel 28:12-18; Isaiah 14:12-17).

- Demons promote false teaching and doctrine in the Church (see 1 Timothy 4:1–5). False teachers appear as angels of light even though they really are workers of Satan (see 2 Corinthians 11:13-15).

- Demons try to lead us away from pure devotion to Jesus Christ and into compromising situations (see Matthew 4:1-11).

- Demons want to discourage and destroy us in spiritual warfare (see Ephesians 6:10-18).

While all these demonic devices may seem overwhelming, there is encouragement: if we are not ignorant of these devices, it is more likely we will defeat Satan and his demonic forces. We need to know who and what we are fighting before we can win the battle. Having noted that, let us now turn our attention to the definition of demonization.

DEFINITION OF DEMON POSSESSION

In the New Testament, both demon invasion and so-called "demon-possession" are more accurately defined as "demonization." Our English translations have improperly translated the Greek *daimonizomai* (meaning "demonization") as "demon-possession." This translation is misleading because it makes it seem as though the demon owns the person. This is simply not the case. Demons do not own anything or anyone. In fact, they belong to God because they are creatures and He is the Creator. Therefore, it is more accurate to say that a person is demonized as a result of being controlled by one or more demons.

Often literature on demons and demonization divides the work of demons into four categories: simple subjection, demonization, obsession, and demon possession by an indwelling spirit. The problem with this classification system is that the Bible knows no such distinctions. It only differentiates between a demon working internally or externally.

In demonization the personality of the demon eclipses the personality of the one being demonized. The demon displays his own personality through the person's body. The control may be overt or covert. There is no indication that the person must be aware of the fact the he is demonized. Demonic control of thought processes seems to be the primary characteristic of demonization.

Consistent with the extreme viewpoints of demonology—eccentricity on the one hand and all-out denial on the other—the concept of demon possession as being bizarre and horrific is not always accurate. Dr. Merrill Unger lists several characteristics of demonized individuals:

- projection of a new personality

- supernatural knowledge

- the ability to speak in unknown languages

- unnatural physical strength

- moral depravity

- deep melancholy and seeming idiocy

- ecstatic or extreme malevolent behavior

- spells of unconsciousness

- foaming at the mouth[25]

Historically, one of the main leaders of studies in demonology in Christian circles has been Dr. Kurt Koch. In Koch's many books on demonology, which have been an inspiration to so many Christian leaders, he lists the following symptoms of demonization:

- a great resistance to prayer

- a reaction to the name of Jesus

- unknown languages[26]

German psychologist Dr. Alfred Lechler lists the following symptoms of demonization:

- a passion for lying and impure thoughts

- restlessness and depression

- compulsion to rebel against God and blaspheme

- excessive sensual or sexual cravings

- a resistance to and hatred of spiritual things

- an inability to pronounce or write the name Jesus

- an appearance of a medium/mystic with clairvoyant capabilities

- an inability to act on Christian counsel

- an inability to renounce the works of the devil

- seizures, spells of unconsciousness, extraordinary physical strength

- speaking in unknown languages

- molestation and pain not connected with illness[27]

Dr. Lechler advises that there must be great discernment between what is psychological and what is demonic. Dr. Unger adds:

> *The new nature bestowed at regeneration constitutes the sphere in which the Holy Spirit works in the believer through his regenerated human spirit. The powers of darkness cannot invade or indwell that holy sanctum. This seems obvious because God's 'seed' (the new nature) remains in the believer alongside the old nature. God's child, therefore, cannot practice sin as a habit (see 1 John 3:9). If he does, he demonstrates himself, says John, to be a member of the devil's family and not of God's family (see 1 John 3:8, 10)... Unfortunately, the term "demon possession" has been commonly used, not to refer only to all cases of demon invasion, but incorrectly to refer only to the basest and most evil enslaving forms, such as those represented by the demoniac of Gadara (see Mark 5:1–20).[28]*

Therefore, demonization is not ownership, as the term

"demon-possession" suggests. Rather, it is influence.

DISOBEDIENCE OPENS THE DOOR FOR DEMONS

Numerous Scripture passages reveal very clearly that a Christian can open the door to demonic invasion and infiltration through disobedience. We are warned in 1 Peter 5:8, "Be sober, be vigilant; because your adversary the devil walks about like a roaring lion, seeking whom he may devour." This is spoken to Christians!

Satan can devour Christians. Dr. Unger writes, "Certainly this conveys the idea that the powers of darkness are able to make a very serious encroachment upon the life of a child of God. In fact, they go so far as to kill the body. How dare a believer ignore this warning or tone down its terrifying implications?"[29] This is why it is so important for us to obey the Lord at all times. It is not that God is a cosmic killjoy. Rather, He wants to protect us from demonic activity and influence. He wants to keep us from being consumed.

The story of Ananias and Saphira (see Acts 5) gives us a glimpse of what happens when someone disobeys God and allows Satan to fill his heart. This husband and wife were, or at least claimed to be, Christians.

Moreover, in 1 Corinthians 5 we read of a man who was involved in incest. He too was a Christian who was handed over to Satan for a time. His disobedience led to demonic activity in his life. In 1 Corinthians 10, Paul speaks of the "thorn in the flesh." It was a messenger from Satan, a demon, sent to torment him.

Additionally, we find the strange case of Saul in the Old Testament (see 1 Samuel). Saul had problems with the flesh and a "wicked spirit." A demon came upon him and tormented him. Although he began his reign in good fashion, Saul's reign and life eventually deteriorated into pride and spiritual rebellion. In

1 Samuel 10:9 we read, "Then it happened when he turned his back to leave Samuel, God changed his heart; and all those signs came about on that day."

We can say with great confidence that Saul was a believer because "God changed his heart." Additionally, we know that God anointed Saul as king over Israel; it would be absolutely inconsistent for God to anoint an unbeliever to rule over His kingdom.

Early in Saul's reign he enjoyed God's blessings on his life. As a result of pride, disobedience, and sin, however, God allowed an evil spirit to trouble him.

Notice 1 Samuel 15:13: "Samuel came to Saul, and Saul said to him, 'Blessed are you of the LORD! I have carried out the command of the LORD.'" This was a lie! Saul had not done all the Lord had commanded him to do. Samuel exposed the lie: "Why then did you not obey the voice of the LORD, but rushed upon the spoil and did what was evil in the sight of the LORD?" *(1 Samuel 15:19).*

In 1 Samuel 15:23 Samuel denounced Saul's actions: "For rebellion is as the sin of divination, and insubordination is as iniquity and idolatry. Because you have rejected the Word of the LORD, He has also rejected you from being king."

The result of Saul's sin and disobedience is recorded in 1 Samuel 16:14, "Now the Spirit of the LORD departed from Saul, and an evil spirit from the LORD terrorized him." First Samuel 16:23 continues the narrative, "So it came about whenever the evil spirit from God came to Saul, David would take the harp and play it with his hand; and Saul would be refreshed and be well, and the evil spirit would depart from him."

What do we learn from Saul's life? We learn that disobedience opens the door to demonic activity in our lives. Dr. Unger notes:

Satan and his minions have no legal right to enter, for a Christian's body belongs only to God by creation and

redemption (see Psalm 100:3; I Corinthians 6:19, 20).
But as a squatter, defined as "one who settles on land
without right or title or payment of rent," a demon can
come in and settle down for a time. He will leave only
if forcibly ejected by faith and prayer on the part of
Christian warriors who know their position in Christ
and use their prayer armour effectively.[30]

Thus, Paul's warning in Ephesians 4:27 stands as a clear reminder of the danger that comes when we allow Satan room to work in our lives. Paul clearly instructs us not to "give place to the devil." The translated word "place" in this passage is interesting. The idea is that we should not give the devil room to act. In other words, do not give the devil room to work in your life. One commentator noted that this would be like leaving a door cracked open in our hearts. When we have some area of sin in our lives that we are unwilling to give up, we leave the door open for Satan to work. Once again, Unger comments:

The claim that the Holy Spirit could not dwell in the
same body with an evil spirit overlooks an important
theological observation. It might with equal cogency
be asked how the Holy Spirit can dwell in our bodies,
which are still possessed of the old nature and therefore
subject to sin. Yet He does because our redemption and
the presence of the new nature.... It must be stressed
that demons cannot indwell a Christian in the same
sense as the Holy Spirit. God's Spirit enters a believer
at salvation, permanently, never to leave (see John
14:16). A demon, by contrast, enters as a squatter and
an intruder and is subject to momentary eviction.
A demon never rightfully or permanently indwells a
saint, as the Holy Spirit does, and a demon can never
have any influence over any part of a Christian's life

that is yielded to the Holy Spirit. (31)

The bottom line is this: Disobedience opens the door to demonic infiltration in our lives.

DOORS FOR DEMONIC INVASION

Demons work in three principle areas to gain entrance into our lives.

1. The works of the flesh—base, human, undisciplined urges. Although we are Christians, we still have to wrestle with the flesh. Our flesh has desires that can carry us away from God. We can choose to bring our bodies under the control of the flesh, or the Spirit. The choice is ours!

Read carefully what Paul wrote to the Galatians: "Now the works of the flesh are evident, which are: adultery, fornication, uncleanness, lewdness, idolatry, sorcery, hatred, contentions, jealousies, outbursts of wrath, selfish ambitions, dissensions, heresies, envy, murders, drunkenness, revelries, and the like; of which I tell you beforehand, just as I also told you in time past, that those who practice such things will not inherit the kingdom of God" *(Galatians 5:19–21).*

This means that Satan will work in our lives when we just "let go"—when we refuse to discipline our human desires. What are these desires?

- *Adultery:* the Greek word is *porneia* from which we get our English word "pornography;" the term refers to illicit sexual behavior.

- *Uncleanness (akatharsis):* a term that was used medically to refer to an infected, oozing wound.

- *Lewdness (aselgeia):* any excess or lack of restraint sexually.

- *Idolatry:* anything we have placed ahead of Christ in our lives.

- *Sorcery (pharamakeia)*: this term is the root of our English word "pharmacy" or "pharmaceutical." It refers to mind-altering drugs.

- *Jealousy (zelos)*: this term is the root of our English word "zeal"; it means the desire to have what someone else has.

- *Dissentions:* the word means "a standing apart."

- *Revelries (komos)*: it means unrestricted revelry; enjoyment that has degenerated licentiousness.

The key word in the verse is practice: "those who *practice* such things" (emphasis added). The word "practice" translates to a participle, the tense of which indicates a durative, ongoing action. It describes a continual and habitual practice of unacceptable things, which indicates that the person doing them is not a Christian. If you commit one of these sins once, it doesn't mean you are not going to heaven. But the continual practice of these sins without repentance or change should give one serious pause to question whether or not he is genuinely saved.

How do we overcome the flesh? We must walk in the Spirit. Paul boldly proclaims, "...Walk in the Spirit, and you shall not fulfill the lust of the flesh" *(Galatians 5:16).*

Every day I ask God to fill me with His Spirit so that I will walk with Him and not fulfill the lust of the flesh. Unger has commented, "It is true of course that the believer has been delivered from the power of Satan and demons. He also has been delivered from the power of sin. But does that mean he may not fall under its power if he does not count on his deliverance? Likewise, he may through his old nature succumb to the temporary control of Satan and demons unless he reckons his deliverance."[32]

Hal Lindsey is also helpful on this point. He writes:

The danger in this concept is that a deed which is actually a part of the flesh, or the old sin nature is attributed to a demon. It is vital that we assign things to their proper cause. There is no "lust demon" per se. Lust is a sin, which comes from the flesh. But there are demons that will use the lust of the flesh to guide us into moral disaster. Satan can take a natural desire and use it, but he is not the originator of it. He capitalizes on something which is already going on in our hearts.[33]

Discipline is the key. We must train our hearts and submit to the spirit. If we do not have any lust in our lives, we leave Satan with nothing to capitalize on.

2. The world's philosophy and influence, which rejects Jesus Christ. Wrong thinking creates bad behavior. The world's battle is for the mind of the believer. Demonic brainwashing is the imposition on the believer of any philosophy or theology that rejects the Lordship of Jesus Christ. Read Romans 12:2 in the Philips translation: "Don't let the world around you squeeze you into its own mold, but let God remold your minds from within."

Paul warns against the anti-God, philosophical systems of the world: "Beware lest anyone cheat you through philosophy and empty deceit, according to the tradition of men, according to the basic principles of the world, and not according to Christ. For in Him dwells all the fullness of the Godhead bodily" *(Colossians 2:8–9).*

3. Demons utilize any habitual sin practiced by believers to gain entrance into their lives. James wrote clearly: "...when desire has conceived, it gives birth to sin; and sin, when it is full-grown, brings forth death" *(James 1:15).*

John echoes a similar theme: "You are of your father the

devil, and the desires of your father you want to do. He was a murderer from the beginning, and does not stand in the truth, because there is no truth in him. When he speaks a lie, he speaks from his own resources, for he is a liar and the father of it" *(John 8:44)*.

DETECTING DEMONIZATION

We have noted that the word *daimonizomai* does not mean to be possessed or owned in the sense in which we understand possessed. It simply means to be demonized, or to be in some way affected by a demon. When a person becomes demonized, he is affected and hindered. Symptoms could include:

- unnatural fear of any sort

- periods of depression

- continual confusion in the mind and inability to allow God's Word to take root in our hearts and minds

- obscenities and profanities assaulting the mind and promoting sensual urges

- prolonged insomnia brought on by spiritual conflict in our lives

- sudden suicidal and murderous urges

- urges to abuse drugs and alcohol while ignoring the danger of these substances

- absolute rebellion to authority and spiritual covering

- marital conflict and unbridled anger

- violent urges, violent auditory suggestions, violent visions

The solution to escaping demonization is simple—not necessarily easy to do, but simple: "Therefore submit to God.

Resist the devil and he will flee from you" *(James 4:7)*.

The authority of God in our lives is a covering that protects us of from the wiles of Satan. We resist demonic attack through the blood and name of Jesus Christ. We increase our faith through studying, reading, and memorizing the Word of God (see Romans 10:17).

CLOSING DOORS TO THE DEMONIC

Demons can work in the life of the believer only two ways:

- when the person opens the door of disobedience through habitual sin

- according to God's permissive will for His purpose (look at the life of Job)

Do you have a door open to the demonic in your life right now? We know we have nothing to fear from demons as long as we are under the authority of Jesus Christ because He has defeated them. Colossians 2:15 states, "Having disarmed principalities and powers, He [Jesus] made a public spectacle of them, triumphing over them in it." MacArthur writes about this verse, "In yet another element of the cross work, Paul tells us that the cross spelled the ultimate doom of Satan and his evil host of fallen angels. While His body was dead, His living, divine spirit actually went to the abode of demons and announced His triumph over sin, Satan, death, and Hell."[34]

Notice also 1 Peter 3:19: "By whom also He [Jesus] went and preached to the spirits in prison." MacArthur is also helpful concerning this point:

> *Between Christ's death and resurrection, His living spirit went to the demon spirits bound in the abyss and proclaimed that, in spite of His death, He had triumphed over them. This (spirits in prison) refers to fallen angels (demons) who were permanently bound*

because of heinous wickedness. The demons who are not so bound resist such a sentence (see Luke 8:31). In the end, they will all be sent to the eternal lake of fire (see Matthew 25:41; Revelation 20:10).[35]

If you are facing demonization in your life, turn to Jesus Christ and submit your life to Him. He is the one—the only one who can save you, redeem you, transform you, and deliver you from the sin that so easily entangles your life.

DISCUSSION QUESTIONS

1. What does the Greek word *daimonizomai* mean? Why is our understanding of this term essential to answering the question, Can a Christian be demon possessed?

2. What are some of the characteristics of those who are demonized?

3. Often times, treatable mental illness has similar symptoms to demonization. How would you discern or help someone else determine if the symptoms are the result of spiritual influences or a medical condition?

4. Is it possible to place undue blame on demons and on satanic influence for the problems and sin struggles in our lives? Why or why not?

5. Why is disobedience an open door for demonization?

6. What are some of the base desires we must keep in check if we wish to escape demonic activity?

7. How can you utterly destroy the attempts of Satan and his demons to establish a stronghold in your life?

8. Do a study of Jesus' interaction with demons in the Gospels. Remember that you are in Him and that He is greater than any demon. Draw near to Him, and they will flee from you.

CHAPTER 5

IDENTIFYING AND ELIMINATING DEMONIC STRONGHOLDS

THE WAR IN THE SPIRITUAL REALM

For though we walk in the flesh, we do not war according to the flesh. For the weapons of our warfare are not carnal but mighty in God for pulling down strongholds, casting down arguments and every high thing that exalts itself against the knowledge of God, bringing every thought into captivity to the obedience of Christ, and being ready to punish all disobedience when your obedience is fulfilled (1 Corinthians 10:3–6).

Above is the key text for our study on identifying and eliminating demonic strongholds in our lives. Read it carefully.

KEY WORDS

We need to focus our attention on several key words in the above passage as we begin our study.

1. Notice Paul writes in verse three "we do not war...." Paul uses a very interesting word for "war" in this passage. It is a military term from which our English word "strategy" is derived. This term was used to describe generals who led their armies into battle. When Paul employed this word, his original hearers would have immediately pictured an organized, formidable military force. We may not always be organized on our side, but Satan is certainly organized on his, and he is indeed a fearsome enemy. He has taken his innumerable host of demons and placed them in the four categories we explored in Chapter 1: principalities, powers, rulers of the darkness of this age, and spiritual hosts of wickedness.

2. Paul writes in verse four, "For the weapons of our warfare...." The word translated "weapons" was used to describe the military hardware needed to carry out battle plans. In Paul's day this would have included swords, bows, arrows, etc. I have noticed that mature Christians do not just recite "party lines" about Christian spirituality. Mature Christians know the weapons necessary to defeat Satan.

In reference to these weapons Paul continues in verse four saying they "...are not carnal but mighty in God...." The strength of our spiritual weapons does not come from us! The victories won with spiritual weapons given to us by God are won because we are mighty in Him.

When people say that they are beaten down and defeated by Satan, we must ask the question, Where is the strength of their weapons coming from? Is it coming from them, or is it from God? The spiritual weapons that we have been granted by God are for His glory.

We glorify God when we become victors in the spiritual battle. When we resist temptation and take the higher road, we bring glory to God. When we lead a "no-compromise" lifestyle, we bring glory to God. We are capable of living this kind of life that brings glory to God because He has given us the spiritual weapons we need to stand strong and victorious in the battle against Satan. Dr. R.C.H. Lenski makes a profound observation:

The absence of the article means that any and all such reasonings are included. They may be impressive philosophies, findings of sciences, or the arguments of the common man with which he tries to satisfy the little thinking that he is able to do. Paul says: "we continue to wreck them." And the engines of divine truth do, indeed, wreck them. The whole course of history is full of these wrecks. It is pitiful to see men trying to repair some of these wrecked reasonings today as if they could afford safe in such repaired redoubts [sic].[36]

Paul also notes (see verse four) that we have been given these spiritual weapons "...for pulling down strongholds."

Here Paul continues his uses of military terminology. The word translated "pulling down" was used to describe military forces that could destroy walls of fortresses by ramming, rock throwing, and undermining.

In Paul's day above the city of Corinth rose a fortified mountain known as the Acrocorinth. This looming hill looked like an ominous fortress. Paul likens the giant hill fortress to the spiritual forces that try to invade our lives. The great preacher and author Warren Wiersbe writes:

There are walls of resistance in the minds of people, and these walls (like the walls of Jericho) must be pulled down. What are these 'mental walls?' Reasoning that is opposed to the truth of God's Word. Pride of intelligence that exalts itself. Paul was not attacking intelligence, but intellectualism, the high-minded attitude that makes people think they know more than they really do (see Romans 12:16).[37]

Paul continues his explanation and exhortation regarding demonic strongholds that afflict us "...casting down arguments...."

Here again, Paul uses yet another military metaphor: arguments are strongholds people erect in their minds to fortify themselves against the invasion of the knowledge of God. Paul says that through these arguments the knowledge of God is prevented from entering our lives. He also says that these arguments, or fortresses, can be cast down and destroyed. The word is in the present, indicating that God's people have continual strength in this battle to demolish fortresses of wrong thinking that can cause wrong behavior. This does not mean that the instant we become Christians God gives us supernatural victory over everything in our lives. It does mean that He will continue to give us victory throughout our Christian lives.

In verse five, Paul continues to paint a vivid picture of the battle in which the Christian is engaged. He explains that through God's might we can cast down false arguments and "...every high thing that exalts itself against the knowledge of God...."

Once again, the language Paul uses is stripped from the world of ancient military combat. The term "high thing" translates the word that denoted a tower or a raised rampart. Brilliant Princeton scholar and theologian Dr. Charles Hodge points out, "Every high thing, every tower or fortress; it is the same word as in verse four. It is a metaphor for thoughts, not people. It is everything that the pride of human reason exalts against the knowledge of God—that is, God's revelation of Himself in the Gospel... The conflict Paul refers to here is that between truth and error, between the wisdom of God and the wisdom of the world."[38]

Both the "stronghold" of verse four and the "tower" ("high place") of verse five are metaphors for intellectual arguments, or for the way the demonic accommodates the reasonings of a disobedient individual. When we become disobedient we conjure excuses for our behavior, and the excuses come from fallen reasoning and intellect. Thus, excuses become strongholds and high places we erect against the knowledge of God. J.B. Philips makes this clear in his translation of 1 Corinthians 10:3–5:

> *The truth is that, although we lead normal human lives, the battle we are fighting is on the spiritual level. The very weapons we use are not human but powerful in God's warfare for the destruction of the enemy's strongholds. Our battle is to break down every deceptive argument and every imposing defense that men erect against the true knowledge of God. We fight to capture every thought until it acknowledges the authority of Christ. Once we are sure of your obedience, we are ready to punish every disobedience.*

Paul says we must strive to bring every thought captive to Christ. The translated word "thought" means either "thought" or "mind." Ultimately, this word points to the way a person thinks. How do we think when doubt, temptation, or disobedience enter our minds? How do we control these thoughts? We control them by bringing them into the captivity of Jesus Christ. We ought to pray each day: Father, help me to have the mind of Jesus Christ today. Father, help me not to think any thoughts that dishonor you today, make it clear to me when I am thinking thoughts that are not pleasing to you and disrupt your peace in my life.

Greek scholar Dr. Robert Gromacki comments, "After ancient cities were conquered, often there were insurrections and attempts to rebuild the destroyed walls. A believer must continually suppress unregenerate, proud thoughts and plans that rebel against holy, spiritual knowledge."[39]

The translated Greek phrase "bringing every thought into captivity" is in the present tense, indicating that the act of taking mental prisoners is in progress. The battle is being won, and the victory is inclusive. This is why memorizing Scripture is so important. When we get thoughts that are not of God we can use memorized Scripture to take those thoughts captive in Christ. Greek scholar Dr. Marvin Vincent makes this excellent observation:

> *The military metaphor is continued; the leading away of the captives after the storming of the stronghold. The campaign against the Cilician pirates resulted in the reduction of a hundred and twenty strongholds and the capture of more than ten thousand prisoners... in pursuance of the metaphor. The obedience is the new stronghold into which captives are led. This is indicated by the preposition into or unto.*[40]

This metaphor suggests that we need to be active in taking carnal strongholds out of our lives and replacing them with godly strongholds gleaned from God's Word. That means we need to have a private prayer time every day.

SPIRITUAL CONFLICT REQUIRES SPIRITUAL WEAPONS

Our spiritual conflict is against the works of our flesh that war against our spiritual nature. What are the works of the flesh? They are the things listed in Galatians 5:19–21:

> *Now the works of the flesh are evident, which are: adultery, fornication, uncleanness, lewdness, idolatry, sorcery, hatred, contentions, jealousies, outbursts of wrath, selfish ambitions, dissensions, heresies, envy, murders, drunkenness, revelries, and the like; of which I tell you beforehand, just as I also told you in time past, that those who practice such things will not inherit the kingdom of God.*

Every one of the sins listed above can be committed by a believer if they deviate from the truth and from obedience to

God. But a believer won't practice these sins habitually because the conviction the Holy Spirit is operating in him and bringing about change in his life. Remember: when we are in obedience to God, we are protected from Satan.

Satan's attacks are subtle, but real. They come as temptations. Let's look at some examples.

Some temptations are easy to recognize. For instance, demons tempt us to hate people who have said hurtful things to us.

Other temptations are harder to discern, for example, idolatry. What does idolatry look like in the life of a believer? In my life, it looked like the Kansas City Chief's football team.

There was a time when I flew into Kansas City every week and rushed to the stadium just to see them play. This doesn't mean that you can't enjoy a football game, or love watching football, but the moment an activity, a person, or a thing becomes more important to you than God, you have slipped into idolatry.

When temptations come into our lives, we must remember 1 Corinthians 10:13, "No temptation has overtaken you except such as is common to man; but God is faithful, who will not allow you to be tempted beyond what you are able, but with the temptation will also make the way of escape, that you may be able to bear it."

God will provide a way for us to escape every temptation that comes into our lives. When facing temptation, we need to ask others to pray with and for us. Ask your spouse or a close friend to pray with you when you are struggling with something.

It's important to highlight the truth that we cannot choose obedience half-heartedly. Sometimes we close the door of disobedience—but not completely. We might leave it slightly open just in case something happens in the future. That is deadly, because the next time temptation comes we can just give the door a little push and it will swing wide open. Temptation and sin work so subtly that we must make sure we close the door hard and fast.

We will always have the ability to open the door to sin. Whenever we choose to open the door to temptation, no matter how old, or mature, or immature we may be as believers, we bring ourselves into a state of disobedience. Opening the door to temptation and sin is disobedience. We can love Jesus with all our hearts and come to church every time it's open and still face the possibility of wrecking everything God has done in our lives by one act of disobedience.

Disobedience is the reason the Church so often lacks power. Many people in the Church have shut and locked the door of disobedience, while others have kept it wide open. When some people in the body of Christ are disobeying Christ's commands, a church will not have the power it ought to have. The Spirit of God will be hindered in the church that has members who have left the door open to rebellion against God.

THINGS DEMONS USE

What things do demons use to work against us?

First of all, they use works of the flesh. We need to make sure we have Galatians 5:19–21 firmly planted in our minds so that we can recognize the works of the flesh as soon as they appear. We cannot accept the self-righteous lie that says, Because I am a Christian, I will never do any of those things. We would be surprised how far and how fast we would fall if we threw the door of disobedience wide open.

Demons, however, use not only works of the flesh, but a whole host of other methods. Look at the list below:

- *Demons use fear.* We must remember the truth of 1 John 4:18, "There is no fear in love; but perfect love casts out fear, because fear involves torment. But he who fears has not been made perfect in love."

- *Demons use guilt.* This is one of Satan's most effective tools; he tempts us to sin and then holds our disobedience up to us and condemns us. What do we do when we are confronted with unfounded guilt and condemnation? Turn to Psalm 130:3 to see: "If You, LORD, should mark iniquities, O Lord, who could stand? But there is forgiveness with You, that You may be feared."

- *Demons use worry.* This is a huge weapon that demons and Satan use against us. They get us to focus on our problems rather than focusing on God and viewing our problems as opportunities to see Him work in us. God has commanded us not to worry (see Matthew 6). Remember what the prophet wrote in Isaiah 26:3, "You will keep him in perfect peace, whose mind is stayed on You, because he trusts in You."

- *Demons use disobedience.* Satan tempts us to ignore the commands of our spiritual leaders and to do what we want to do instead. Paul writes to the Church at Thessalonica, "And if anyone does not obey our word in this epistle, note that person and do not keep company with him, that he may be ashamed" *(1 Thessalonians 3:14).*

- *Demons use infiltrated minds.* We must be aware of the teaching, music, and other media we allow to shape our thoughts and hearts. We must always keep Philippians 2:5 before our minds, "Let this mind be in you which was also in Christ Jesus."

- *Demons use undisciplined bodies.* We need to exercise and eat healthy so that nothing controls us. Paul wrote, "But I discipline my body and bring it into subjection, lest, when I have preached to others, I myself should become disqualified" *(1 Corinthians 9:27).*

- *Demons use the works of the flesh.* We saw this in Galatians, and Paul emphasizes it again in Romans 7:23, "But I see another law in my members, warring against the law of my mind, and bringing me into captivity to the law of sin which is in my members."

SPIRITUAL WEAPONS THAT COUNTER ATTACKS

We will close this study on a positive note by looking at strategies and spiritual weapons to counter the things demons use to establish strongholds in our lives. Take a look at the weapons below:

- *The Word of God:* "And take the helmet of salvation, and the sword of the Spirit, which is the Word of God" *(Ephesians 6:17).*

- *Prayer:* "Praying always with all prayer and supplication in the Spirit, being watchful to this end with all perseverance and supplication for all the saints" *(Ephesians 6:18).*

- *The Holy Spirit within us:* "And I will pray the Father, and He will give you another Helper, that He may abide with you forever" *(John 14:16).*

- *A disciplined mind:* "Finally, brethren, whatever things are true, whatever things are noble, whatever things are just, whatever things are pure, whatever things are lovely, whatever things are of good report, if there is any virtue and if there is anything praiseworthy—meditate on these things" *(Philippians 4:8).*

- *The Belt of Truth:* "Stand therefore, having girded your waist with truth..." *(Ephesians 6:14a).*

- *The Breast Plate of Righteousness:* "...having put on the breastplate of righteousness" *(Ephesians 6:14b).*

- *Spiritual Shoes:* "...and having shod your feet with the preparation of the Gospel of peace" *(Ephesians 6:15).*

- *The Shield of Faith:* "...above all, taking the shield of faith with which you will be able to quench all the fiery darts of the wicked one" *(Ephesians 6:16).*

- *Helmet of Salvation:* "And take the helmet of salvation, and the sword of the Spirit, which is the Word of God" *(Ephesians 6:17).*

Now that we've looked at the spiritual weapons briefly, let's review what we have learned from 2 Corinthians 10:3–5.

WHAT 2 CORINTHIANS 10:3–15 TEACHES

We have gleaned five key points from 2 Corinthians 10:3-15:

- Whether we admit it or not, we are in a spiritual battle every day of our Christian lives. The days we are most likely to fall are the days when we forget that truth.

- God has provided every weapon we need to counter every method of attack we will face.

- Our victory begins when we pull down every mental stronghold that attempts to embed itself into our minds and influence our behavior.

- The most difficult "high thing" or problem in our lives can be overcome through Jesus Christ.

- It all starts with our thoughts. We must remind ourselves that the battle always begins in our minds; therefore, we must always be alert to examine our thought lives.

How do we identify and eliminate demonic strongholds in our minds? By searching our thought life for fortresses and strongholds that open the door to disobedience. When we eliminate these strongholds, we eliminate the open doors of disobedience. With the doors of disobedience shut, we are free from demonic influence and able to serve Jesus Christ with all of our heart, mind, soul, and strength.

DISCUSSION QUESTIONS

1. In the first section of this chapter we examined Paul's use of military terminology in 2 Corinthians 10:3–6. What do these metaphors teach us about the reality of the spiritual battle we are in as followers of Jesus Christ?

2. What are the works of the flesh? How do they allow demons to gain a stronghold in our lives?

3. Take some time this week to read Galatians 5. Ask God to help you to see where you have given in to the flesh, and ask Him to help you walk by the Spirit, specifically in those areas.

4. In this chapter we listed a number of things that demons use to gain strongholds in our lives. To which of these are you most susceptible? How can you construct godly fortresses to prevent Satan from taking ground in those areas?

5. What are some weapons that God has given us for defending ourselves against the attacks of Satan? Are you making use of these weapons?

CHAPTER 6

THE AUTHORITY OF THE BELIEVER

The lessons I am about to share in this chapter I learned in less than a minute on one of the most memorable days of my life.

It was a Thursday afternoon at the church. I had just left a meeting with one of the other pastors and was returning to my office. As I was walking I heard a car roar into the parking lot. When I turned to see what was happening, I saw the car swing into a parking space and squeal to a stop just outside the office entrance. An elderly woman and her 40-year-old daughter jumped out and rushed into the lobby. As they approached me, I could tell something was wrong with the daughter. I thought jokingly to myself, *This woman looks possessed*. Little did I know it was no joke: the woman was demon possessed.

They continued walking toward me, and I noticed the daughter's eyes were wide open and her pupils were dilated. Her movements were stiff and unnatural.

As I approached them, they rushed up to me and the elderly woman said, "Where is Jerry Johnston? We need to talk with Jerry Johnston!" I responded, "I'm Jerry. Can I help you?"

Almost as if she didn't hear what I said, she pleaded, "I need to talk with Jerry Johnston about my daughter."

I responded, "Is there some way I can pray with you?"

Then she looked me in the eye and said, "My daughter is demon possessed, and we need prayer for her because we heard that you prayed for a girl who was demon possessed in Oklahoma and that she was delivered."

I took a deep breath and said, "Wait here for just a moment." I set two chairs out in the hall and asked them to have a seat.

I regained my composure, and went to talk to another pastor. "There's a demon possessed woman in the hall," I told him.

At first he laughed and thought I was joking, but then realized I was serious. "Are you ready? Let's go," I said, with more confidence than I felt.

I must admit I was scared. This woman was much larger than I was, and I envisioned myself getting beaten up by the demon in her.

We prayed over her for about 15 or 20 minutes in the best way we knew how. While we were praying, she shook every once in a while and her eyes rolled back in her head, but when we finished praying, she blinked and seemed a little more normal.

I learned an important lesson that day: as Christians with Jesus Christ in our lives and the Holy Spirit in our hearts we have no need to fear demons, and more than that, we have authority over demons and the satanic realm in which we live.

BIBLE 101

The text we will examine now is Mark 9:14–29. Before we begin studying this text, it's important to know who the author was, who the writer was, who the book was written to, and why the book was written. Knowing these facts will help us interpret this passage with more accuracy.

The author of the book of Mark is the apostle Peter. John Mark, also the Mark who traveled with Paul on his missionary journeys, recorded Peter's words in the Gospel of Mark. According to tradition, John Mark spoke with Peter who told him the Gospel narrative from his perspective.

John Mark recorded Peter's words in the Gospel of Mark. He wrote the book to the Jews to demonstrate that Jesus was a servant. A lot of Jews were religious during that time, but few knew what it meant to be a servant.

THE SITUATION – MARK 9:14–15

Let's read the first part of Mark 9:14-15. It describes the situation: "And when He came to the disciples, He saw a great multitude around them, and scribes disputing with them. Immediately, when they saw Him, all the people were greatly amazed, and running to Him, greeted Him" *(Mark 9:14–15).*

The situation was unique, but not because there was a demon possessed person involved. It was unique because Jesus was there! Isn't it interesting that any situation looks completely different and unique when Jesus is involved? Everything can change in an instant when Jesus is there.

Where had Jesus been before he arrived on the scene of this unique situation? He had just been on a mountain where Peter, James, and John witnessed His transfiguration. While Jesus' mountaintop experience was incredible, He knew that people needed Him at the base of the mountain. When He arrived on the scene among them, the people were "greatly amazed." They were greatly amazed just to be in His presence!

Perhaps you are tempted to think that today Jesus is not in the world anymore so our situation is different. Our situation is not unique because Jesus is in the world today through believers. We are His body, and when demons see Jesus' body, the Church, they see Jesus.

THE POSITION OF THE BELIEVER

Since we are part of Christ's body as believers, we are His presence in the world. It is essential that we understand our position in Him. Romans 8:28–30 powerfully communicates what our position is:

> *And we know that all things work together for good to those who love God, to those who are the called according to His purpose. For whom He foreknew, He also predestined to be conformed to the image of His Son, that He might be the firstborn among many brethren. Moreover whom He predestined, these He also called; whom He called, these He also justified; and whom He justified, these He also glorified.*

Notice the word "glorified." It is in the past tense in our English translations. The past tense in English renders a past, passive verb in Greek. The past, passive means that the action has already taken place and that it was done to us by someone else. This means that God has already glorified us as believers. It is not something we have done to ourselves, or that is waiting to happen. The action has already been completed by God. He glorified you and me the moment we trusted Jesus as our Saviour.

Yet God is not the only one who sees us as glorified. Satan sees us as glorified also. Satan sees our position and authority in Christ. He knows that our spiritual citizenship is not on earth (see Philippians 3:20); it is in heaven with our great God and Saviour Jesus Christ.

God does not view time in the same way we do. From God's perspective, all things are in the present. Second Peter 3:8 makes this abundantly clear: "But, beloved, do not forget this one thing, that with the Lord one day is as a thousand years, and a thousand years as one day."

Our salvation is therefore complete in His eyes. Paul reiterates this to the Ephesian believers: "In Him you also trusted, after you heard the Word of truth, the Gospel of your salvation; in whom also, having believed, you were sealed with the Holy Spirit of promise, who is the guarantee of our inheritance until the redemption of the purchased possession, to the praise of His glory" *(Ephesians 1:13–14)*.

Paul argued that God sees the salvation of believers as complete even now. God views time much the same way as a person in a helicopter views a parade. If you are on the ground watching the parade, you see one section passing at a time. However, if you are in a helicopter, you see the beginning and the end of the parade. The whole parade is visible all the time. J. Vernon McGee is helpful on this point. He writes, "I would like to remove the word 'after' from this verse (see Ephesians 1:13) because these are not time clauses. They are what is known in the Greek as genitive absolutes, and they are all the same tense as the main verb. It means that when you heard and you believed, you were also sealed: it all took place at the same time."[41]

The moment God saved us, He saw us in heaven, and so did Satan. Satan knows that sin no longer has power over us if we live according to the Spirit rather than according to the flesh. The moment we are saved, God sees us with the same righteousness, the same authority, and the same eternal destination as Jesus Christ. William Barclay points out:

> *The helplessness of the disciples was a first-rate opportunity to belittle not only them but their Master. That is what made the situation so delicate, and that is what makes every human situation so delicate for the Christian. Their conduct, their words, their ability or inability to cope with the demands of life, are used as a yardstick, not only to judge them, but to judge Jesus Christ.*[42]

If that statement is true, what do your co-workers think

about Jesus from what they see of Him through your actions? I don't think any demon will see more of Jesus in you than your kids see in you. How much Jesus do they see in your life? How about your husband or wife? Or your business partners? A demon will only see as much Jesus in your life as others do.

THE STORY – MARK 9:16–18

"And He asked the scribes, 'What are you discussing with them?' Then one of the crowd answered and said, 'Teacher, I brought You my son, who has a mute spirit. And wherever it seizes him, it throws him down; he foams at the mouth, gnashes his teeth, and becomes rigid. So I spoke to Your disciples, that they should cast it out, but they could not'" *(Mark 9:16–18)*.

Jesus had come down from the mountain and evaluated the situation. He saw that the disciples were a little embarrassed because they had been unable to cast the demon out of the man's son.

Who was present in this story?

- Nine of the disciples were present (the other three arrived with Jesus).

- The scribes were there. The scribes were the Bible experts of their day. They copied and taught the law. They were the theological experts of the Jewish religion. These men followed Jesus around waiting for Him to do something that broke the Jewish law.

- People were there. A crowd had gathered. Many of them were familiar with the demon-possessed boy.

It's interesting to note that the father failed to mention God in his search for help. Notice also that he did not address Jesus as Messiah or Son of God, but as "teacher." There were many "teachers" in Jesus' day. Jesus certainly was a great teacher, but He was more: He was God. The father, however, did not recognize this at first. He wanted the service Christ offered without being a servant of Christ.

All too often, we approach Jesus the same way. We want His service, but we are unwilling to serve him. Hank Hanegraaff notes this phenomenon in his book *Christianity In Crisis*:

In recent years, multitudes who name the name of Christ have adopted a wildly distorted perception of what it truly means to be a Christian. Perhaps even more alarming, millions more have been kept from seriously considering the claims of Christ because they perceive Christianity as a con and Christian leaders as con artists.... The true Christ and the true faith of the Bible are being replaced rapidly with diseased substitutes.... This cancer has been triggered by a steady diet of 'fast-food Christianity'—The unsuspecting have been called not to love the Master, but to love what is on the Master's table.[43]

When we tell people about Jesus, we must keep in mind that He said, "Follow me," not, Accept me. Jesus did not invite us to a party in heaven. He invited us to a life of discipleship. He told the disciples to take up their crosses and die with Him that they might gain life.

This man wanted Jesus' service. But notice who else was on the scene—a group who he didn't approach for help: the scribes. He asked the disciples—a group of uneducated men—to help heal his son, but he did not ask the scribes. The scribes had a lot of religion, but they were not servants. They did not seek to help people.

There is a big difference between having religion and having Jesus. A lot of churches are like scribes. They will tell you everything you want to know intellectually about the Gospel, but they refuse to serve.

How much of a servant are you to people at church and the people you work with? How much of a servant are you to your spouse; to your kids? What kind of Jesus do people see in your attitude toward serving others?

Church is not just for receiving a good message on Sunday. Church is for serving, and serving is giving.

Erwin McManus noted that 60 percent of Americans are overweight because they take in more calories than they burn. He then argued that 90 percent of the American Church is spiritually overweight because they take in and take in, but never give out. Jesus calls us to be like the disciples who, even though uneducated and untrained, knew what it meant to serve.

THE SHORTCOMING – MARK 9:19

"He answered him and said, 'O faithless generation, how long shall I be with you? How long shall I bear with you? Bring him to Me'" *(Mark 9:19).*

The faithlessness of that generation was its shortcoming. What type of people made up the generation that Jesus denounced for their faithlessness? Jesus likely had three groups in mind:

- *The disciples:* He was frustrated with them because they had not understood, or truly believed, what He had told them.

- *The scribes:* He was frustrated with them because they had searched the Scriptures, but they hadn't understood who He was and therefore continued to harass Him.

- *The people who were watching what was going on.* He was frustrated with them because they had come to Him for help without acknowledging that He was God.

Through this text Jesus is talking to everyone who is not a Christian, and to every Christian who does not have enough faith to do what He has commanded them to do. This text clearly demonstrates that the beginning of any spiritual failure is a lack of faith. Conversely, we also see that the beginning of any spiritual success is the presence of faith.

THE SPIRIT – MARK 9:20–22

"Then they brought him to Him. And when he saw Him, immediately the spirit convulsed him, and he fell on the ground and wallowed, foaming at the mouth. So He asked his father, 'How long has this been happening to him?' And he said, 'From childhood. And often he has thrown him both into the fire and into the water to destroy him. But if You can do anything, have compassion on us and help us'" *(Mark 9:20–22).*

The power of the demonic spirit that tormented this boy is seen in two words: "convulsed" and "wallowed." The idea of the translated Greek word, "convulsed," is that the boy was shaken so violently that he was nearly torn in two. Secondly, he wallowed. The present active tense of the Greek verb indicates that it was a violent, continual, painful rolling around on the ground. Notice that this happened to the boy often, and the purpose was the boy's destruction.

Satan does not want to make us feel bad, or trip us up. He wants to destroy us! Peter said clearly that Satan is a roaring lion seeking to devour believers. However, we must always remember that He who is in us is greater than he who is in the world. Satan is powerful. But Jesus is more powerful.

THE SUPERNATURAL POWER – MARK 9:23–29

"Jesus said to him, 'If you can believe, all things are possible to him who believes.' Immediately the father of the child cried out and said with tears, "Lord, I believe; help my unbelief!"

When Jesus saw that the people came running together, He rebuked the unclean spirit, saying to it, 'Deaf and dumb spirit, I command you, come out of him and enter him no more!' Then the spirit cried out, convulsed him greatly, and came out of him. And he became as one dead, so that many said, 'He is dead.' But Jesus took him by the hand and lifted him up, and he arose. And when He had come into the house, His disciples asked Him privately, 'Why could we not cast it out?' So He said to them, 'This kind can come out by nothing but prayer and fasting'" *(Mark 9:23–29)*.

At the end of verse 22, the father of the demon-possessed boy stated, "Jesus if you can do anything, have compassion on us." Jesus' answer to his question in verse 23 would be better translated, "What do you mean if I can? Of course I can, but you have to believe that I can."

Why do we need faith? Because "Without faith it is impossible to please God," *(Hebrews 11:6)*. James 1:6 also affirms this: "But let him ask in faith, with no doubting, for he who doubts is like a wave of the sea driven and tossed by the wind." Charles Spurgeon explains the result of a failure of faith. He wrote:

> *Let us look in the same direction personally, and we shall see that unbelief is an alarming and criminal thing; for it doubts the power of Omnipotence, the value of the promise of God, the efficacy of Christ's blood, the prevalence of his plea, the almightiness of the Spirit, the truth of the Gospel; in fact, unbelief robs God of His glory in every way, and therefore it cannot receive a blessing from the Lord.*[44]

Are we robbing God of glory in some area of our lives where we do not believe Him? Are there areas we struggle with everyday, but do not really believe that God can help us overcome? We will not have victory until we choose to believe God for who He is and what He has said. Mark 9:24 is one of the most amazing verses in the Bible because the man confesses his unbelief and asks Jesus to help him believe: "Immediately the father of the child cried out and said with tears, 'Lord, I believe; help my unbelief!'" Faith—even small faith—is effective in spiritual warfare.

Remember what Jesus said: "...for assuredly, I say to you, if you have faith as a mustard seed, you will say to this mountain, Move from here to there, and it will move; and nothing will be impossible for you" *(Matthew 17:20)*.

THE PRACTICALITY OF THE BELIEVER'S POSITION

While the believer's position is in Heaven, their life is to be lived on Earth. Paul wrote to the Philippian believers, "Only let your conduct be worthy of the Gospel of Christ, so that whether I come and see you or am absent, I may hear of your affairs, that you stand fast in one spirit, with one mind striving together for the faith of the Gospel" *(Philippians 1:27)*.

The Bible reminds us many times that the Earth is not our true home as believers. We are merely travelers passing through. We are ambassadors for the King to all nations, but one day we will return home to Him. Until we return, He has given us some guidelines for living in this foreign world that is not our home.

The first guideline is the Mosaic Law. The second is the Sermon on the Mount. The third set of guidelines is the teaching found in the New Testament epistles (see Romans to Revelation). Below is a sampling of verses from the New Testament that summarizes well the practicality of the believer's position:

- "I beseech you therefore, brethren, by the mercies of God, that you present your bodies a living sacrifice, holy, acceptable to God, which is your reasonable service" *(Romans 12:1)*.

- "Rejoice always, pray without ceasing, in everything give thanks; for this is the will of God in Christ Jesus for you. Abstain from every form of evil" *(1 Thessalonians 5:16–18, 22).*

- "But the fruit of the Spirit is love, joy, peace, longsuffering, kindness, goodness, faithfulness, gentleness, self-control. Against such there is no law" *(Galatians 5:22–23).*

- "I, therefore, the prisoner of the Lord, beseech you to walk worthy of the calling with which you were called, with all lowliness and gentleness, with longsuffering, bearing with one another in love, endeavoring to keep the unity of the Spirit in the bond of peace" *(Ephesians 4:1–3).*

- "Therefore do not be unwise, but understand what the will of the Lord is. And do not be drunk with wine, in which is dissipation; but be filled with the Spirit, speaking to one another in psalms and hymns and spiritual songs, singing and making melody in your heart to the Lord, giving thanks always for all things to God the Father in the name of our Lord Jesus Christ" *(Ephesians 5:17–20).*

- "Therefore take up the whole armour of God, that you may be able to withstand in the evil day, and having done all, to stand" *(Ephesians 6:13).*

- "If then you were raised with Christ, seek those things which are above, where Christ is, sitting at the right hand of God. Set your mind on things above, not on things on the earth" *(Colossians 3:1–2).*

If you put these seven verses into practice in your life, your position as a believer will be strong and secure. However, putting them into practice is not easy. Remember the narrative we just looked at above: Jesus cast the demon out of the child, but before it left, it threw him to the ground and convulsed him.

Deciding to follow Christ, obeying the verse above, and abandoning sinful habits is almost never easy, and in fact, can be quite painful. But Jesus came that we might be set free from sin and be enabled to serve God. He commands us to cut those things out of our lives that keep us from following Him with all our heart, soul, mind, and strength.

In addition to applying the verses listed above, another key to the believer's authority is prayer. The *Wycliffe Bible Commentary* notes, "Unbelief and prayerlessness are sure to result in spiritual impotency."[45] Prayer is essential because while Satan's demons are not nearly as powerful as God, they are still very powerful, and believers cannot afford to be spiritually impotent when facing their attacks. The Bible gives believers three instructions concerning prayer:

- *Pray without ceasing.* Praying without ceasing is a life lived in constant dependence on God. "Praying always with all prayer and supplication in the Spirit, being watchful to this end with all perseverance and supplication for all the saints" *(Ephesians 6:18).* "Pray without ceasing" *(1 Thessalonians 5:17).*

- *Pray believing.* This may include prayer for greater belief: "Immediately the father of the child cried out and said with tears, 'Lord, I believe; help my unbelief!'" *(Mark 9:24).*

- *Pray in Jesus' name.* "And whatever you ask in My name, that I will do, that the Father may be glorified in the Son" *(John 14:13).*

Before you confront demonic forces, however, first carefully note the advice William Barclay gives: "Here is a warning thought. The disciples had been equipped with power direct from Jesus, but they had not nurtured power with prayer, and power had vanished.... We keep [it] when we enrich [it] by continual contact with the God who gave [it]."[46]

Jesus told the disciples that the demon they were unable to cast out on their own would only come out by prayer and fasting. Fasting is essential to the spiritual authority of the believer. The key to fasting however, is not food: it is focus. Only with the most extreme focus on God can the believer overcome the powers of Satan. *The Thomas Nelson Study Bible* comments, "Fasting may help focus one's energies on the resources available in our great God."[(47)]

Oswald Chambers makes this insightful remark:

"Why could we not cast him out?" The answer lies in a personal relationship to Jesus Christ. This kind can come forth by nothing but by concentration and redoubled concentration on Him. We can ever remain powerless, as were the disciples, by trying to do God's work not in concentration on His power, but by ideas drawn from our own temperament. We slander God by our very eagerness to work for Him without knowing Him.[(48)]

Giving our lives to God requires our utmost concentration. As I read this passage from Oswald Chambers, I thought of a professional golfer on the golf course. When he is preparing to putt, he looks at the ball from all the possible angles and then bends down on his knees behind the ball and looks at the shot again. He redoubles his concentration.

If we really desire to take our lives back for Christ's sake, we need to get on our knees just like the golfer does when he is preparing to putt. We need to pray and concentrate on God. We need to redouble our concentration on God and His Word. The bottom line is this: the authority of the believer rests in Christ, the action of the believer resides with the believer. The power of Christ comes into our lives when we empty ourselves of our own power.

DISCUSSION QUESTIONS

1. What is the position of the believer? Are believers residents of Heaven, Earth, or both? What are the implications of your position?

2. Is our salvation in progress, complete, or both? Explain your answer.

3. What is the significance of Jesus' command to "Follow me" as opposed to Accept me?

4. What are our guidelines (listed above) for living as travelers? Select one of the verses from the list of seven and commit it to memory this week.

5. What are the three instructions given to believers concerning prayer?

6. What is the essence of the idea of fasting? What practical things can you do to increase your concentration on God and His Word?

CHAPTER 7

HOW GOD USES DEMONS FOR HIS PURPOSES

Have you ever met a Christian who "lives like the devil" —a Christian who is evil, engaged in immoral and inappropriate behavior? Have you ever wondered what has happened to people like that? We will explore this question as we study how God uses demons for His purposes.

Several years ago a woman competed in the World Championship Ironman Triathlon. This grueling athletic competition consists of a 2.4 mile swim followed by a 112 mile bike ride, immediately followed by a 26.2 mile run. The entire race is 140.6 miles of excruciating endurance performed in less than ten hours. Shortly before the race this woman called and asked me to pray with her. Her prayer request was not just that she would win the race with her muscles, but that she would win the race with her mind also.

Similarly, we win spiritual battles we face when our minds know all the facts and appropriate the truth of God's Word in every area of our lives. Most people who fail to complete marathons and triathlons do not fail because their bodies are incapable of finishing, but because their minds lose focus, and they are unable to push themselves to victory. Since the battlefield on which the spiritual battle is fought is the mind, if we keep our minds in check, our bodies will follow their leading in submission to God, His will, and His Word.

The passage we will now examine is 1 Corinthians 5.

Paul wrote the letter of 1 Corinthians to believers who lived in Corinth, which was at the time one of the main cities in Greece. The country of Greece is divided into two parts. The southern part of the country is attached to the northern part by a very narrow, four-mile long isthmus. The city of Corinth was situated in the middle of that isthmus to the south, on a commanding plateau. Julius Caesar had rebuilt the city, and many retired Roman soldiers lived there.

At the time of Paul's letter, Corinth was the political capital of Greece as well as the centre of its commercial and intellectual life. All the north and south overland traffic, including to and from Athens, had to pass through Corinth. Similar to New York City in our context, Corinth was a place where people from many different cities and nations met and interacted. From a spiritual point of view, I believe they were also drawn to the city because of the vices that were practiced there.

The city of Corinth was a successful entertainment centre. The Isthmian Games, second only in popularity to the Olympic Games, were held in Corinth. The city boasted a 20,000 seat outdoor amphitheatre and a 3,000 seat indoor theatre where plays and musical performances were held. The Temple of Diana, one of the many temples in the city, employed 1,000 "priestesses" (temple prostitutes) who went throughout the city every night enticing men of the city and visiting travelers. The corruption in this city was so well-known that the name "Corinthian" was equated with the grossest immorality and drunken debauchery. Eventually, the noun was turned into a verb meaning "to act like a Corinthian." In summary, the Corinthians had a cavalier attitude toward sexual promiscuity, to say the least.

Much of the behaviour that was commonplace in Corinth 2,000 years ago is still common in many parts of the world today—including America. Unfortunately, just as today, the Church in Corinth was not immune to the vices of its surrounding culture. Paul wrote the letter of 1 Corinthians to exhort the Church at Corinth to deal with sexual immorality that believers not only tolerated, but exalted.

DELIVERING A BELIEVER TO SATAN

The specific situation that Paul addressed in 1 Corinthians 5 concerned a man—a Christian brother in the Church—who was involved in an incestuous relationship with his father's wife. Note carefully in different translations what Paul instructed the Church to do about this situation *(1 Corinthians 5:4–5)*:

- *New King James:* "In the name of our Lord Jesus Christ, when you are gathered together, along with my spirit, with the power of our Lord Jesus Christ, deliver such a one to Satan for the destruction of the flesh, that his spirit may be saved in the day of the Lord Jesus."

- *Amplified:* "In the name of the Lord Jesus Christ, on the man who has committed such a deed. When you and my own spirit are met together with the power of our Lord Jesus. You are to deliver this man over to Satan for physical discipline [to destroy carnal lusts which promoted him to incest], that [his] spirit may [yet] be saved in the day of the Lord."

- *New American Standard:* "In the name of our Lord Jesus, when you are assembled, and I with you in spirit, with the power of our Lord Jesus, I have decided to deliver such a one to Satan for the destruction of his flesh, so that his spirit may be saved in the day of the Lord Jesus."

We glean several important facts from this passage. Let's look at them.

THE INCESTUOUS MAN

1. Everybody in the Church knew about his immoral behavior, and they seemed to condone it! The local church knew what was going on with this man and his incestuous relationship, but as is the case in many of our churches today, they refused to confront sin. This fact is obvious from 1 Corinthians 5:1, 9–11:

> *It is actually reported that there is sexual immorality among you, and such sexual immorality as is not even named among the Gentiles—that a man has his father's wife! … I wrote to you in my epistle not to keep company with sexually immoral people. Yet I certainly did not mean with the sexually immoral people of this world, or with the covetous, or extortioners, or idolaters, since then you would need to go out of the world. But now I have written to you not to keep company with anyone named a brother, who is sexually immoral, or covetous, or an idolater, or a reviler, or a drunkard, or an extortioner—not even to eat with such a person.*

Paul had instructed the believers at Corinth to stay away from believers who did not obey the Word of God. They were, of course, supposed to associate with unbelievers just as Jesus did, to share the Good News with them, however, they were not to associate with sinning believers. J. Vernon McGee writes:

> *They did not carry out this procedure in Corinth. This was a case of compromise with evil. The Church in Corinth was compromising itself by compromising with this evil. There are certain things about this case that we need to note. This case was an acknowledged situation which had no need of proof. This was not a matter of gossip or hearsay. Paul would never have brought up something like this if it had simply been a*

rumour.[49]

Dr. John MacArthur adds:

The fact that it was "actually reported that there is immorality among you," indicates it was common information and should have been as shocking to them as it was to Paul. The church had been carefully taught by Paul and other ministers. The Corinthian believers were well grounded in Christian doctrine and morals.... But sadly, the problems Paul addresses in this chapter were not new to the Corinthians, and was being tolerated...[The] Corinthian church had a general reputation for immorality, and word of it had come to Paul more than once.[50]

It is a sad day when sin is rampant in the Church and yet does not cause repulsion. It was exactly in that position that the Church at Corinth found itself approximately 2,000 years ago.

Too many pastors and preachers today also tolerate far too much sin in their own lives and in the lives of their congregations. We need pastors and church leaders today who will stand up for the truth and faithfully proclaim the Word of God, no matter the cost!

2. The specific sin was incest—the man was living with his stepmother and having sex with her. Paul states in 1 Corinthians 5:1, "It is actually reported that there is sexual immorality among you, and such sexual immorality as is not even named among the Gentiles—that a man has his father's wife!"

Paul exclaimed that this type of sexual immorality was not even common among the Gentiles. He used the Greek word *porneia* (immorality) from which we derive our English word "pornography" and which refers to any illicit sexual activity. The present tense verbs in this passage indicate the relationship was somewhat permanent and ongoing. The young man was living with his stepmother and probably attending church at Corinth with her. Perhaps their relationship had already caused the woman to divorce her husband, the young man's father.

3. The Corinthians had a twisted view of grace and were proud of this odd, sinning couple attending their church. Notice what Paul writes in 1 Corinthians 5:2, "And you are puffed up, and have not rather mourned, that he who has done this deed might be taken away from among you?" The Corinthian Church had such a distorted view of grace that they rejoiced and were proud of the immorality that was among them. This is the situation in so many churches today, where "diversity" and "tolerance" are exalted at the cost of holiness and godliness.

4. Paul instructs the entire Church to deliver the man to Satan. Paul's command is clear in 1 Corinthians 5:5, "Deliver such a one to Satan for the destruction of the flesh that his spirit may be saved in the day of the Lord Jesus." The translated word "deliver" in this passage is a strong term indicating the judicial act of sentencing—of handing over for punishment. The sentence passed on this sinning believer was a scary one indeed! To be handed over to Satan is no light punishment. Practically, this command meant that the Church at Corinth was to give this man to the devil. He was to be placed outside the protective fold of the Church where Satan and his demons could have free access to him.

The translated word "destruction" is also very interesting. It too is a strong term. The noun form of this verb occurs later in 1 Corinthians 10:10 where it is translated to "the destroying angel." It may even refer to death. I believe that some Christians have died prematurely because they strayed from God's will, and He sovereignly chose to take them home early.

J. Vernon McGee's comments are helpful. He writes:

Paul is telling them to meet together, and if this brother will not forsake his sin, they are to deliver him over to Satan. That is a tremendous statement. Does he really mean that? He said it; apparently he meant it. This is something the Word of God teaches. Do you realize there is a danger of our feelings and our fanaticism to which some people are inclined; but in our churches today we do have certain men and women who are hurting the cause of Christ? I believe we have the right to ask God to deliver them into the hands of Satan, to be dealt with, so that they won't hurt and harm the body of Christ. I pray that God will deliver certain men over to Satan to let him give them a good workout. It will either bring them to God or it will reveal the fact that they are not genuine believers at all... I think we have a right to pray that prayer.[51]

John MacArthur also offers insight:

The destruction of the flesh indicates that the incestuous man in Corinth would eventually die unless he repented of his sin. We are not told of the specific affliction, disease, or circumstance, but his body was on the way to destruction in a special disciplinary way. If he kept sinning, his life would end before he otherwise would have died. He would go to heaven, because he was a believer; but he would go before he should have gone. To protect His Church, the Lord would have taken him early.[52]

Charles Hodge adds: "So that the sinful nature [or "the flesh"] may be destroyed. Many people understand this to mean the destruction of his corrupt nature, so that the end in view is merely a moral one. But as 'flesh' here is contrasted with spirit, it most naturally means the body. The man was delivered to

Satan that his body might be afflicted, in order that his soul might be saved."[53]

5. Scripture suggests that, although painful, the process worked and the man did repent. In 2 Corinthians 2:6–8, Paul seems to indicate that the man of 1 Corinthians 5 had repented and was ready to rejoin the fellowship of believers. Paul writes, "This punishment which was inflicted by the majority is sufficient for such a man, so that, on the contrary, you ought rather to forgive and comfort him, lest perhaps such a one be swallowed up with too much sorrow. Therefore I urge you to reaffirm your love to him."

Regardless of whether the same person is in view here as mentioned in 1 Corinthians 5, the principle is the same: when a sinning believer repents, we must welcome him back into the fellowship.

CHURCH LEADERS DELIVERED TO SATAN

In 1 Timothy we find another example of people being turned over to Satan. Paul writes, "This charge I commit to you, my son Timothy, according to the prophecies previously made concerning you, that by them you may wage the good warfare, having faith and a good conscience, which some having rejected, concerning the faith have suffered shipwreck, of whom are Hymenaeus and Alexander, whom I delivered to Satan that they may learn not to blaspheme" *(1 Timothy 1:18–20)*.

We need to observe several key points concerning this passage.

1. Hymenaeus and Alexander, originally leaders and teachers in the Church at Ephesus, were delivered to Satan by Paul. Paul writes, "As I urged you when I went into Macedonia—remain in Ephesus that you may charge some that they teach no other doctrine" *(1 Timothy 1:3)*.

Why did Paul make this statement? We find the answer

in 1 Timothy 1:6–7: "From which some, having strayed, have turned aside to idle talk, desiring to be teachers of the law, understanding neither what they say nor the things which they affirm."

It is likely these teachers were mixing law and grace—confusing the true nature of the Gospel.

2. Paul himself had rejected and excommunicated these two false teachers. He warned Timothy to allow "no other doctrine." In Greek, this is a compound word made up of two words that mean "of a different kind" and "to teach." It suggests teachers who teach another kind of doctrine—one that was foreign to the Gospel revealed by God in and through Jesus Christ and His Word.

3. Hymenaeus is mentioned later with another false teacher, Philetus. In Paul's second letter to Timothy, he wrote, "And their message will spread like cancer. Hymenaeus and Philetus are of this sort."

4. Hymenaeus and Alexander had rejected faith and a good conscience. The word "reject" means to "thrust away" or "refuse." False teachers are always revealed by their rejection of biblical truth.

5. Paul delivered the two men to Satan to "learn." This word means "to train through physical punishment, not to blaspheme." This is the same word used in Luke 23:16, 22 to speak of Pilate's scourging of Christ and in 1 Corinthians 11:32 of those who suffered illness or death for abusing the Lord's Table (communion).

OTHER EXAMPLES OF DELIVERING TO SATAN

These examples are not the only ones in Scripture where God uses Satan to accomplish His purposes. Consider the following:

- *Job:* God gave Satan access to Job. Job's reaction

ultimately proved the genuineness of his faith and defeated Satan's attempt in his life (see Job 1:1–5, 6–12, 13–22, 42:1–6).

- *Jesus Christ:* After fasting for 40 days, Jesus was turned over to Satan for heavy temptation and proved obedient, revealing the power of the Word of God and the sinlessness of His nature (see Matthew 4:1–11).

- *Paul:* This rare Christian leader who impacted the entire world for Christ could have become very proud. God allowed Satan access to Paul to keep him humble and dependant (see 2 Corinthians 12:1–10).

- *Peter:* Satan desired to destroy Peter in the same manner he does every believer. Jesus' prayers for Peter intervened and set limits on Satan's attempted destruction (see Luke 22:31–33).

- *Tribulation Saints:* These particular saints will sing a song of praise unknown by believers because of what they will be allowed to suffer and because of their ultimate deliverance from Satan by God (see Revelation 7:9–15).

- *Judas Iscariot:* He was handed over to Satan, committed the grievous sin of betraying the Son of God, and ended up committing suicide (see Matthew 27:3-5).

WHY GOD USES DEMONS

Why does God choose to use demons? The answer represents the heart of this chapter of study. Here are some reasons:

1. For physical punishment in hope of restoration. When believers engage in activities that they know they ought not to be engaged in, at a certain point God will turn them over to Satan for their own good.

2. To remind other believers of the severity of

discipline enacted by God and the Church, when a true Christian sins (the fornicator of Corinth and false teachers in Ephesus).

3. To reveal the character of true faith during trials (Job).

4. To humble arrogant Christians and remind them of their spiritual dependency (Peter).

5. To take unique, effective Christians to a new level of maturity and usefulness (Paul) in God's laboratory of character building.

6. To reveal and mercilessly judge false Christians and false teachers (Judas).

7. To remind us that God is sovereign and all-powerful, and that He is the author and finisher of our faith. God sets limits on Satan and uses him for His purposes any time He wants. Hebrews 12:2 states, "Looking unto Jesus, the author and finisher of our faith, who for the joy that was set before Him endured the cross, despising the shame, and has sat down at the right hand of the throne of God."

It is therefore important for us to examine our lives and see if we are making any compromises that could give Satan access to our minds. Are we living in a way that would cause God to hand us over to Satan? Is your marriage or your family suffering because you have allowed Satan access to your life? Are you doing what God wants you to do? If you are not, take a moment right now to confess your sin and ask Him to help you obey God's Word more completely.

DISCUSSION QUESTIONS

1. Why is the mind such an essential part of the study of spiritual warfare and demonic oppression?

2. What are the five facts that we need to understand about the situation in 1 Corinthians 5?

3. Are there areas of sin in your life, or in the life of your church that you are "proud of"? How can you change your thinking about these sins to reflect God's view of them?

4. Why is handing someone over to Satan or excommunicating him or her from the church such a devastating punishment?

5. How should believers respond when a sinning believer repents? Are there people in your life whom you have refused to receive back even though they have repented?

6. List and discuss some of the examples from Scripture of how God uses demons in people's lives. List and discuss the different ways God uses demons for His purposes.

CHAPTER 8

ON THE OFFENSIVE AGAINST DEMONIC SPIRITS

THE SWORD OF THE SPIRIT

"... and take the sword of the Spirit, which is the Word of God," *(Ephesians 6:17b).*

One thing is certain: if you are going to be a fruitful, prayerful, joyful Christian who seeks to be used by God, you are going to be the target of demonic attack.

The preceding chapters gave us an overview of demons: their origin, character, deceptive strategies and future. This information, if we are not careful, can leave us in a defensive spiritual posture. No one wins a battle just playing defense.

In Chapter 1 we learned that demons —innumerable numbers of them intent on destroying the Christian—are segregated into four diabolical categories of evil.

We discovered that the word "wrestle" the way Apostle Paul employs it in Ephesians 6:12, means "hand-to-hand combat." Imagine the scene: two enemies engaged in a grueling attack to kill one another have lost their weapons and are left using only their hands to destroy. This is the etymology of the word "wrestle."

I have now been in ministry more than 35 years and observed many pastors and evangelists who have burned out, or lost their anointing and the power of God due to sin. In the first decade of my evangelistic career my wife Cristie and I experienced extreme grief due to the suicide of our pastor. Outwardly he was very successful with a church of nearly 4,000 members. Inwardly this troubled pastor and dear friend was losing the battle that had led him into a long-term, secretive, adulterous affair with the wife of one of his closest parishioners. In my spirit, I had sensed something was wrong in the months prior to his self-inflicted death. The Holy Spirit's joy had left him. Pride had set in. He treated his wife rudely. Cristie and I were deeply concerned.

One fateful, bleary March day his son called me and told me his dad had shot himself in the head. There is no question in my mind this pastor was under severe demonic attack and had lost the battle.

THE ATTACK AGAINST PASTORS

My doctoral dissertation at Acadia University's Divinity College in Wolfville, Nova Scotia, was devoted to the theme of why an inordinately high number of pastors and Christian workers succumb to adultery, physical and emotional breakdown, and the ruin and premature end of their ministries.

Pastoral moral failure is at catastrophic levels. Of more than 600,000 clergy in the United States, studies reveal that some 60,000 to 75,000 pastors act on sexual temptations with their own congregants. An astounding 165–205 pastors fail morally every day—i.e., six to nine pastors commit sexual indiscretions per hour. Every six to ten minutes a pastor falls morally in the United States, not to mention the high numbers of failing clergy in Canada.

Every month some 1,600 pastors in United States churches quit or resign from their jobs and nearly 20 percent of clergy suffer stress or burnout.

Clergy sexual misconduct exceeds that of all other professionals including psychiatrists, psychologists, and physicians. Surveys reveal that some 100,000 pastors report fighting sexual attraction and temptation with respect to church congregants.

One out of every two pastors in full-time vocational ministry quits during the first five years of service. Studies reveal that churches terminate one in every four pastors. The average tenure of a minister who serves in the role of "church pastor" is a brief 3.8 years.

PASTORING – A HAZARDOUS OCCUPATION

Why do pastors quit? Why are they so discouraged?

The office of the pastor is on the list of the top ten occupational hazards for heart disease. In one survey, 75 percent of pastors reported that their marriages are unfulfilling—a common precursor to inappropriate clergy sexual misconduct.

Many churches are in conflict. Cloaked demonic forces have divided believers within Christian assemblies, and consequently churches have little, or no impact on their communities. Churches in constant conflict eventually destroy their pastors. Every year congregational conflict and dissension lead to the demise and dismissal of thousands of clergy.

Pastors who preach and teach the Word of God are under *constant* demonic attack. Discerning church members must pray unceasingly for their pastor(s) and for the unity and harmony of their church fellowship. Remember, every time the church comes together for corporate worship, demons come too, and will use any mechanism possible to hinder the work of the church.

Paul admonished believers about the reality of demons and their power and warned: "Therefore take up the whole armour of God, that you may be able to withstand in the evil day, and having done all, to stand" *(Ephesians 6:13).*

PATHWAY TO PEACE AND CLARITY

How did Matthew Fontaine Maury discover the paths in the sea? He was nicknamed "Pathfinder of the Seas," "Father of Modern Oceanography and Naval Meteorology" and later, "Scientist of the Seas," due to the publication of his extensive research, especially in his book *The Physical Geography of the Sea* (1855), the first extensive and comprehensive book on oceanography. His discoveries have been of inestimable help to navigators. Oceanography owes a great debt to the books of Matthew Fontaine Maury, yet Maury acknowledged a debt to the Bible for some of his scientific findings concerning oceanographic direction.

One day when Maury was ill, his son read Psalm 8 to him. When the boy read the eighth verse, his father asked him to repeat it: "The birds of the air, and fish of the sea, and all that swim the *paths of the sea.*"

When the boy finished, the great scientist declared: "If there are paths in the sea, I am going to find them." Today great oceangoing vessels follow paths in the sea marked out by Matthew Fontaine Maury who believed they were there because the Bible said so.

Amazingly, the Bible gives precise direction regarding actual paths in the sea—highways designed for travel. The Bible can also illuminate your heart and mind to the spiritual warfare you face, and simultaneously provide you with a path to peace and clarity in the battle. What a profound book the Bible is!

IGNORANCE OR IMMERSION

I meet too many Christians who are ignorant of the Bible. The Word of God, the Bible, is crucial to the spiritual battle in which you are engaged. You must read it daily, meditate on its rich truths, memorize it for spiritual guidance, and most important, be ready to use it as a sharp, offensive sword against the demonic attack that comes upon you.

For many years I have read my Bible through from Genesis to Revelation. My dad reads his Bible, cover to cover, every ten-and-a-half weeks! If you read five chapters of the Bible in the morning, ten every night and 20 chapters on Sunday, you can read the Scriptures through in two-and-a-half months. Perhaps that's too difficult for you. But remember, it only takes 20 minutes of Bible reading per day to read from Genesis to Revelation in one year. You and I have 20 minutes!

Demons hate the Bible because of its power. In Matthew chapter four we read how Jesus responded to Satan's temptation by quoting the Word of God. Eventually Satan fled because he could not stand up to God's inspired Word.

We experience the same victory if our minds are immersed in biblical truth on a daily basis. The word "Bible" means "books" and there is a reason. Consider the number of "books" in the Bible and their contents:

- 39 books in the Old Testament; 27 books in the New Testament

- 66 books in the Bible (Have you read them all? They contain thousands of promises for you to claim.)

- 929 chapters in the Old Testament; 260 in the New Testament

- 1,189 total chapters in the Bible (Have you read them all?)

- 33,214 verses in the Old Testament; 7,959 verses in the New Testament

- 41,173 verses in the Bible (Have you read them all?)

- 593,493 words in the Old Testament; 18,253 words in the

New Testament

- 774,746 total words in the Bible (Have you read them all?)

ARMOUR FOR OFFENSE AND DEFENSE

In Ephesians 6:14-17 Paul mentions six pieces of spiritual armour God has given true believers in Christ who desire to be successful at defeating the inevitable demonic attacks they face.

Five of these pieces are defensive in nature—designed to protect you as you wage war against "principalities, against powers, against the rulers of the darkness of this age, against spiritual hosts of wickedness in the heavenly places" *(Ephesians 6:12).*

The sixth piece is offensive—designed to cut down illicit spirits that wage war against you.

DRESSED FOR BATTLE

A believer must "put on" the full "armour of God"—utilize all six pieces of armour, both defensive and offensive. Again, we read: "Therefore take up the whole armour of God that you may be able to withstand in the evil day ..." *(Ephesians 3:13).*

Pastors who fall morally do not have on the "whole" armour of God.

Parents who are in a quandary about leading their children have not put on the "whole" armour of God.

Fathers protect their families when they put on the "whole" armour of God daily.

Discerning Christians are disciplined. They put on the "whole" armour of God as they make time for daily Bible reading and prayer. Why? Because they know demonic spirits abound and observe our fruitfulness for Jesus Christ.

The six pieces of armour mentioned in our Bible text must be worn at all times. What are these six pieces of spiritual armour? Let's look at them in light of the armour Roman soldiers wore at the time God gave Paul this text.

A Roman soldier in full gear was chained to Paul for two years when he penned, under the inspiration of the Holy Spirit, the book of Ephesians. In my mind I see Paul carefully studying the armour on the Roman soldier who guarded him as the Holy Spirit illuminated each piece of armour and revealed its spiritual significance.

ARMOUR FOR DEFENSE

Each piece has immense significance to believers in Jesus Christ because we are at war with demonic spirits. In a war a soldier needs protection and a weapon for attack. The passage in Ephesians chapter six delineates the various protective parts of this armour:

- *Belt of Truth:* "Stand therefore having girded your waist with truth..." *(Ephesians 6:14a).*

- *Breastplate of Righteousness:* "...having put on the breastplate of righteousness" *(Ephesians 6:14b).*

- *Shoes:* "...and having shod your feet with the preparation of the Gospel of peace" *(Ephesians 6:15).*

- *Shield of Faith:* "Above all, taking the shield of faith with which you will be able to quench all the fiery darts of the wicked one" *(Ephesians 6:16).*

- *Helmet of Salvation:* "And take the helmet of salvation..." *(Ephesians 6:17a).*

- *Sword of the Spirit:* "...and the sword of the Spirit, which is the Word of God" *(Ephesians 6:17b).*

The believer must put on these six pieces of spiritual armour every day. Fiery darts come at various moments from the wicked one against the child of God, but when a believer has the wisdom to have a quiet hour before God each morning, to read the Bible and spend time in prayer, spiritually these six pieces of armour are applied to his or her life.

A WEAPON FOR OFFENSE

A Roman soldier used two types of swords in battle.

1. Short sword: The sword Paul referred to in Ephesians 6:17b in Greek is called *machaira*. The word described a short sword used for precision in stabbing, wounding or killing the enemy. This short sword was six to 18 inches long and was commonly used in up-close, hand-to-hand combat.

2. Broad sword: A large, broad sword, in Greek *rhomphaia,* was long and heavy and measured three to four feet in length. It was waved at the enemy indiscriminately. This large sword was used by Roman cavalrymen to split the skull, or decapitate the enemy. It could be used by the Roman soldier, but not nearly with the precision he could demonstrate in attacking his enemy with the short sword.

Paul teaches us a vital spiritual lesson with his selection of the word that represents a short, very sharp sword the Roman soldier used effectively in battle. He stresses that this kind of sword was used when the battle was mercilessly intense.

This is exactly the kind of contest in which we ourselves engage when our minds are tempted to become tainted by impurity. When demons plant ideas of anger, revenge, impurity, and rebellion in our minds, we are in a very close and personal engagement with them. Just like the Roman soldier did, we need to use the short sword.

The short sword, a physical weapon in the hands of a Roman soldier, is a spiritual weapon of offense in our hands. It is indeed very interesting in a spiritual sense to realize that this short sword represents the Word of God. Hebrews 4:12 compares the Word of God to a sword because it is sharp and able to pierce the inner man just as the short sword pierced the body. We must "put on" the Word of God along with the rest of God's armour:

- "For the Word of God is living and powerful, and sharper than any two-edged sword, piercing even to the division of soul and spirit, and of joints and marrow, and is a discerner of the thoughts and intents of the heart" *(Hebrews 4:12).*

- "And the sword of the Spirit, which is the Word of God" *(Ephesians 6:17b).*

Charles Hodge reminds us that this sword of the Spirit is the sword that the Holy Spirit gives. Yes, the Holy Spirit gave us the Word of God! That is why we accept it as God's authoritative truth:

- "All Scripture is given by inspiration of God, and is profitable for doctrine, for reproof, for correction, for instruction in righteousness, that the man of God may be complete, thoroughly equipped for every good work" *(2 Timothy 3:16-17).*

- "Knowing this first, that no prophecy of Scripture is of any private interpretation, for prophecy never came by the will of man, but holy men of God spoke as they were moved by the Holy Spirit" *(2 Peter 1:20-21).*

- "But the Holy Spirit also witnesses to us; for after He had said before ..." *(Hebrews 10:15).*

The Holy Spirit endued Bible writers with the ability to give us the very mind of God in the Holy Scriptures without error in the original texts they wrote through his inspiration. He quickened them.

The Holy Spirit brings us to salvation by convicting us of sin, unrighteousness and judgment to come. He illuminates the Word of God to our mental and emotional understanding.

People who have not received Jesus Christ as their Lord and Saviour do not understand spiritual truths because they do not have the Holy Spirit to give them revelation: "But the natural man does not receive the things of the Spirit of God, for they are foolishness to him; nor can he know them, because they are spiritually discerned. But he who is spiritual judges all things, yet he himself is rightly judged by no one" *(I Corinthians 2:14-15)*.

No wonder unbelievers are under the deception of Satan and his demons!

Conversely, the Holy Spirit constantly works in believers reminding us of God's promises in His Word that we have read, meditated upon, and memorized. During spiritual conflict with demonic spirits, the Holy Spirit brings the specific word(s) of God to our understanding just as He did for Jesus during His great temptation. We are then able to cut down illicit spirits by quoting, singing, meditating on, and standing on the Word of God. Demons flee when we wisely apply God's Word to every situation, doubt, problem and challenge in our lives.

A spiritually mature believer takes every demonic doubt and temptation back to the Word of God and conquers it with the words, "It is written!" But, you also have to know *where* "it is written" to stand against demonic spirits.

Here are some examples from my life when using the "short sword" of God's Word with precision worked for me.

There have been times when a demon has come to me unseen and shot a fiery dart of doubt into my mind questioning God's care or love for me. On other occasions there have been moments when the most rude or vile thought has invaded my mind. Because I have spent immeasurable time in the Bible, I know instantly where these thoughts are coming from. In those moments of spiritual weakness I quote the precise Scripture that applies to the situation against the demon(s) harassing me.

The Armour of God

The Apostle Paul, inspired by God, wrote a letter to the church of Ephesus from a Roman prison. As he wrote, Roman soldiers guarding the prison walked about in the armour of first century legionary.

A CLOSER LOOK

Helmet
The iron helmet was forged from one piece of metal and lined with leather. Crests made of dyed horsehair indicated rank. Plates hung down along the cheeks and another plate protected the back of the neck and shoulders.

Breastplate
The iron or bronze scaled armour was built in four sections to cover each shoulder and side of the chest. The plates were sewn to a stiff leather vest, which was put on like a jacket before the front plates were tied with leather straps.

Sword
The sword was carried on the right side and hung from the belt or a leather strap over the shoulder.

Belt
The leather belt was tied around a wool tunic. Connected bronze plates hung from the belt to protect the soldier's groin area.

Shield
The curve was created using three bonded layers of thin wood strips. Covered by linen or leather, the shield was painted according to legion. A bronze rim covered the rounded edges as additional protection.

Sandals
Thick leather soles, embedded with hobnails or bits of rock for increased traction, were tied to the feet with numerous leather straps.

Scripture: English Version Standard Version

Copyright 2008 Logos Bible Software/R. Rolfe

ARMOUR OF LEGIONARY	ARMOUR OF GOD
Galea (Helmet) Protected head and neck from enemy attacks	**Helmet of Salvation** "…and take on the helmet of salvation…" Ephesians 6:17a
Lorica Segmentata (Breastplate) Guarded vital organs	**Breastplate of Righteousness** "…and having put on the breastplate of righteousness…" Ephesians 6:14b
Gladius (Sword) Powerful offensive weapon in the hand of a skilled soldier Waving It served as a word of warning to the enemy	**Sword of the Spirit, Word of God** "…and the sword of the Spirit, which is the Word of God…" Ephesians 6:17b
Cingulum (Girdle or Belt) Supports sword, dagger and bronze apron Worn at all times, even without other armour pieces	**Belt of Truth** "Stand therefore, having fastened on the belt of truth…" Ephesians 6:14a
Scutum (Shield) Overlapping shields allowed soldiers to advance together Shield was used to defend the entire body, including the back	**Shield of Faith** "In all circumstances take up the shield of faith, with which you can extinguish all the flaming darts of the evil one…" Ephesians 6:16
Caligae (Sandals) Fit for both marching and fighting Became more comfortable with constant wear	**Readiness/ Preparation of the Gospel of Peace** "…and, as shoes for your feet, having put on the readiness given by the Gospel of peace." Ephesians 6:15

I quote specific verses that are my "short sword" of the Spirit out loud and combat the demonic harassment. And, guess what? It works!

The Word of God is indeed that powerful because it is inspired by the Holy Spirit. That is why the Bible teaches, "Finally, my brethren, whatever things are true, whatever things are noble, whatever things are just, whatever things are pure, whatever things are lovely, whatever things are of good report, if there is any virtue and if there is anything praiseworthy—meditate on these things. The things which you learned and received and heard and saw in me, these do, and the God of peace will be with you" *(Philippians 4:8-9).*

At other times demons have tried to destroy my emotional stability by tempting me to worry about the many trials in my life. Evil spirits whisper in my ear, Jerry, God has forgotten you. Something horrible is going to happen to you. You better start worrying about this situation, or person.

I have always known these thoughts are not from the Lord, but I have spent many sleepless nights letting them agitate my mind until the Lord reminds me how to expel these demonic spirits from my thought-life by quoting God's Word. I get my spiritual sword out and start the offensive against the demons that have been dispatched to hinder and hurt me. I have lost count how many times I have quoted the following Bible verse to my spiritual foes: "Be anxious for nothing, but in *everything* by prayer and supplication, with thanksgiving, let your requests (notice they are plural—a recognition that we have many needs) be made known to God; and the peace of God, which surpasses all understanding, will guard your hearts and minds through Christ Jesus" *(Philippians 4:6-7).*

Equally, we must be aware of misunderstanding or misapplying God's Word. Deception occurs when we claim the promises of God without meeting the spiritual qualifications.

For example, our thinking can become warped when we twist Scripture to our personal, selfish agenda. Oddly, this was the tactic that Satan displayed when he misquoted God's Word in his attempt to get Jesus to sin. "For it is written" *(Luke 4:10),* he said. Strange, coming from the lips of Satan! Yet Satan uses this tactic successfully today.

We live in a time when pastors equivocate the Word of God in their deceptive sermons and lead people who are not grounded in the Scriptures astray. These false ministers use Bible words without their accurate meaning. They are false prophets and pastors who are praised by men, and yet follow Satan's example quoting just enough Scripture to deceive. These ministers are led by demons.

David Koresh, for example, was led astray by demons when he misquoted Scripture and led everyone in his cult to their death along with him. Jim Jones misquoted Scripture and led hundreds of people in his People's Temple in Jonestown, Guyana, to commit suicide.

Here are some Scriptures that reveal this tactic:

- "But there were false prophets among the people, even as there will be false teachers among you, who will secretly bring in destructive heresies, even denying the Lord who bought them, and bring on themselves swift destruction. And many will follow their destructive ways, because of whom the way of truth will be blasphemed" *(2 Peter 2:1-2).*

- "Having a form of godliness but denying its power. And from such people turn away!" *(2 Timothy 3:5).*

- Jesus half-brother, Jude, wrote: "For certain men have crept in unnoticed, who long ago were marked out for this condemnation, ungodly men, who turn the grace of God into lewdness and deny the only Lord God and our Lord Jesus Christ" *(Jude 4).*

- John cautioned: "If anyone comes to you and does not bring this doctrine, do not receive him into your house nor greet him; for he who greets him shares in his evil deeds" *(2 John 10-11)*.

IT'S ALL IN YOUR HEAD

After I received Christ in 1973, my Aunt Sara taught me the importance of memorizing Scripture. It is impossible to memorize Scripture without meditating on Scripture. God's Word, committed to memory in my teenage years, revolutionized my thinking.

Prior to my salvation I was a suicidal druggie. By the time I entered college I had memorized more than 1,000 verses from the Bible. My focus was Paul's epistles, which represent more than 2,000 verses of the New Testament. I audio-recorded an entire book of Paul's and then listened to it over and over again. As I memorized entire books of the New Testament I entered the dates I completed them on the inside cover of my New Testament.

Since then I have studied God's Word for more than 35 years and have completed a Master of Divinity and a Doctor of Ministry degree. I have learned that many verses of Scripture specifically address the varied challenges and temptations we face as Christians.

When Paul wrote "the sword of the Spirit, which is the Word of God" *(Ephesians 6:17)*, he did not use the typical word *logos* for "Word." Instead, he employed the word *rhēma*, meaning "that which is spoken"—a statement, or more exactly a specific word.

For instance, when a demon sends a fiery dart of worry to your mind, quote out loud, "Be anxious for nothing, but in everything by prayer and supplication, with thanksgiving, let your requests be make known to God" *(Philippians 4:6)*.

When demonic foes cause you to question why God allows problems and difficulties in your life, quote aloud, "And we know that all things work together for good to those who love God, to those who are called according to His purpose" *(Romans 8:28)*.

In other words, use *specific* words of God against *specific* attacks demons launch against you. Then watch temptations subside as demons flee and challenges are put in their proper perspective with an infinite God on the throne of your mind. I am convinced this is what Paul is teaching in Ephesians 6:17. We should use the Bible as a spiritual "machine gun" when necessary to cut down every argument and deception of evil spirits.

Often we wonder why we are so susceptible to demonic attack and so easily overcome with anxiety, depression, and temptation. The answer is, we are not spending enough time in the Word of God.

D.L. Moody, an exceptional evangelist in the 1800s, personally led more than 70,000 people to Christ. More than one million people came to faith in Christ in Moody's evangelistic crusades. Mr. Moody had a personal conviction that he would not allow a 24-hour period go by without witnessing individually to someone. God honoured his evangelistic compassion.

Moody was quoted as saying, "I prayed for faith and thought that some day faith would come down and strike me like lightning. But faith did not seem to come. One day I read in Romans 10:17, 'So then faith comes by hearing, and hearing by the Word of God.' I opened my Bible, and began to study, and faith has been growing every since."[54]

Spend time in the Bible every day. Learn hundreds of Scripture verses by memory. Quote the specific Word of God to every demonic spirit who comes to assault you mentally and emotionally. The Bible is your "short sword" and it guarantees your victory.

Harold Ockenga was the great pastor of Park Street Church in Boston who brought Billy Graham to town when his ministry was just beginning to mushroom. Ockenga wrote:

At the believer's conversion he enters as a soldier into what John Bunyan called "The Holy War." No soldier has entered a grimmer, more difficult and dangerous war. Salvation as purchased by Christ through His death on the Cross, with all the attendant, heavenly blessings is ours, yet a terrible spiritual conflict rages between the time of His decisive victory on Calvary over the prince of this world and our final redemption. The conflict is not between the good and bad influences of our nature, or between the good and bad elements in the world, but between the believer and super-human enemies who must be met with supernatural strength.[55]

One of my favorite Bible commentators, John Phillips from England, reminds us:

...modern man is in much the same plight as 17th century man. In 1665 London was in the grip of the great plague. People were dying by the thousands— faster than they could be buried. Corpses were stacked like cordwood outside stricken houses and were carted away to hastily dug pits on the outskirts of the city. Business came to a halt. Court disbanded. People fled London, taking the disease with them.

Nobody knew the cause of the plague. The most common notion was that air caused it, so people sealed up their homes to keep the contaminated air outside. They burned noxious material in their fireplaces to help drive out the deadly air. Out of ignorance they disregarded the most basic rules of sanitation and hygiene. Open sewers ran down the streets. Rats and vermin multiplied, and their fleas spread like the plague. But the people were unable to see any link between the unsanitary conditions and the spread of the plague. If someone were to go back to 1665 and say that bacteria spread the plague the people would have laughed at them. They would not have believed that there were germs so small that they could not see them with the naked eye, or that millions of germs could be found in a drop of ditch water. People knew nothing about germs or viruses. They would have laughed scornfully at anyone who would try to explain the real source of their troubles. Since germs could not be seen, smelled, touched, heard, or tasted, no one suspected that they could have caused the plague.[56]

How similar to our day! People today do not believe in evil spirits—demons. They say if they can't see them, there is no way they can possibly exist. What a mistake! People scoff at the idea that evil spirits, ruthless in their hatred for mankind, are tirelessly dedicated to keeping people in bondage, addiction, depression, sin, and shame. To deny this fact is to deny the Bible's claim.

Why are record numbers of people killing themselves? Recently, I presided over the graveside funeral of a precious 16-year-old young man who hung himself. His parents came home and found him hanging. His death left them in a state of shock. Kyle gave no warning signs whatsoever. Scores of young people crowded around his coffin and they would not leave even though we had concluded.

Jesus said to the religious elite of His day, "You are of your father the devil, and the desires of your father you do. He was a murderer from the beginning, and does not stand in the truth, because there is no truth in him. When he speaks a lie, he speaks from his own resources, for he is a liar and the father of it" *(John 8:44)*.

Demonic spirits lie to our youth and entice them to commit suicide. Yes, I believe in mental illness, but I also believe very firmly in demonic suggestion, possession, and oppression.

Why are so many people addicted to drugs, alcohol, sex, pornography, gambling, and a host of other ills? These are well-worn tools in the treasure box of the demonic to enslave men and women.

God's Word warns that demons are at work in our world today. Our adversary is not "flesh," and "blood," rather it is demonic spirits. Therefore, our weapons must be spiritual, not carnal. We do not have a physical, visible enemy. We cannot see the devil or his faithful cohorts—demons. But, I can assure you they are present in your life and mine. These demons have worked masterfully through people.

The great 17th century Puritan writer William Gurnall wrote the 1,200 page classic book, *The Christian in Complete Armour: A Treatise of the Saint's War Against the Devil.* Very wisely, Gurnall in this book identifies six situations when demons attempt to destroy the Christian. Please make special note of them.

1. When the Christian is newly converted. And, in particular when the new Christian sins.

2. When the Christian is afflicted. When things go well, demons frequently leave us alone. However, when we go through times of affliction, as all God's children do, demons readily come to suggest that God has abandoned us, or that we are not really His children.

3. When the Christian has achieved some notable success. Shortly after Peter made his majestic, inspired confession to Jesus: "You are the Christ, the Son of the Living

God" *(Matthew 16:16)*, our Lord had to rebuke him with the words, "Get behind me Satan" *(Matthew 16:23)*, because he succumbed to demonic suggestion and tried to dissuade Jesus from going to the cross to die for our sins.

4. When the Christian is idle. We all remember David, when he should have been in battle, idly watching Bathsheba. Just a few minutes of idle thrill and sensation brought a terrible toll of grief, death and regret to the great warrior king.

I must admit I try to stay as busy as possible in the Lord's work. Often people say to me, "Jerry, you should slow down and relax." Honestly, I don't listen. I want to stay busy. I have heard too many stories of lackadaisical pastors playing endless golf games, taking appointments with the opposite sex alone, and playing the fool by getting into serious trouble. My only down time is with my wife and family. Years ago my Aunt Sara taught me, "Idle hands are the devil's workshop."

5. When the Christian is isolated from other believers. This is why we should be faithful in our church attendance, tithing, and serving in the local church. Every time you miss a church service, fail to serve and give, you take one small step backward spiritually. This is a mistake. Stay faithful. Get your kids out of bed and keep them faithful to church.

6. When a Christian is dying. Yes, death is beautiful for the believer who is ready. Far too often I have been at the bedside of believers who were caught by unexpected illness and disease and were not ready. Regret and despair often characterize their disposition. Stay ready to meet the Lord in the air (the Rapture), or at any moment. Live by the phrase that M.R. DeHaan popularized, "Perhaps Today." If I *live* ready, I will be able to *die* ready!

Let's now study the other significant pieces of spiritual armour that make us ready and prepare us for the spiritual contest in which we are constantly engaged.

DISCUSSION QUESTIONS

1. Since Paul understood the word "wrestle" to mean "hand-to-hand" combat, how should we interpret and apply Ephesians 6:12 to our lives?

2. Why is pastoring a "hazardous occupation"? How can members of a congregation help their pastor in his battle?

3. Explain how knowledge of God's Word can help you in your battle against the demonic.

4. Evaluate your personal situation. What circumstances might you be facing that have been engineered by enemy spirits?

5. What steps can you take to overcome the work of the enemy in your life?

CHAPTER 9

YOUR EVIL DAY

"Therefore take up the whole armour of God, that you may be able to withstand in the evil day, and having done all, to stand" *(Ephesians 6:13).*

Tsunamis are the most destructive force of nature. A tsunami is a towering ocean wave caused by an earthquake, landslide, or a volcanic eruption underwater. A tsunami wave can reach about 100 or more feet above sea level. The biggest wave was recorded in 1958, in Lituya Bay, Alaska. It was 1,640 feet above sea level. No one could run away from that!

A tsunami wave can travel about 500 miles per hour, equivalent to the speed of a jet airliner, but there is an oddity surrounding it. You will notice it if you are on a boat deep out in the ocean.

The oddest thing about a tsunami is that it won't hit you when you are far out in the deep because it travels underwater. In the deep sea a tsunami's height might only be about one meter (three feet). As a result a tsunami is often barely visible in the deep sea, which makes its detection very difficult.

The worst thing about a tsunami, therefore, is our inability to know when it's coming, and once it hits, our inability to stop it.

Tsunamis have an extremely long wavelength (distance between the crest, or top of one wave to the crest of the next one) of up to several hundred miles. The period, or time between two successive waves, is also very long—about an hour in deep water.

In addition, tsunamis can savagely attack coastlines causing devastating property damage and loss of life. The large tsunami waves that crash onto shore push a massive amount of water above regular sea level ahead of them. This mass of water, called run-up, causes tremendous damage inland.

When a tsunami begins, water pushes upward, and the impact of gravity forces it to speed toward land. The word "tsunami" is Japanese and means "Harbour Wave" (*Tsu—* harbour; *Nami*—wave). Earthquakes, landslides, volcanic eruptions, explosions, and even the impact of cosmic bodies, such as meteorites, can generate tsunamis. They are most likely to happen in the Pacific Ocean due to the large amount of undersea seismic activity.

Even though tsunamis are rare in the Indian Ocean, the worst tsunami in history was recorded there on December 26, 2004. It hit the west coast of the Indonesian Island of Sumatra. It caused an underwater earthquake 9.0 in magnitude, and its waves traveled more than 3,000 miles before they hit. One witness said the first wave sounded like three freight trains. According to reports, the destruction it caused was similar to 23,000 Hiroshima-type atomic bombs. The catastrophic result was a death toll of 250,000 people.

Scientists warn that in about a decade there will be another tsunami in this same troubled region. It is predicted to be the worst one in history. Oceanographers reached that conclusion after investigating the 700-year history of earthquake activity near West Sumatra. Researchers found imprints on the shallow coral reefs in the region of the tsunami's origin. The findings reveal that the area had witnessed multiple earthquakes during 700 years, and a September 2007 earthquake had opened an ancient rift in the coral reefs along the 700-km stretch of the "Sunda mega thrust." This reef had been intact for 50 years until that quake.

Why are we discussing tsunamis in a study on demonology? There is a reason.

SPIRITUAL TSUNAMIS

All of us as Christians, during our journey, face very unique moments when a spiritual tsunami hits us. Often it can happen during extremely trying circumstances that test us to our very limits. For example, your son or daughter may become rebellious and start going in the wrong direction. Your marriage may begin hemorrhaging with conflict. You may be struggling to shake an addiction to drugs, alcohol, obesity, anger, or depression. Similar to a tsunami, these trials come our way undetected. This is what I call your "evil day." Evil days are special periods of intense, satanic, spiritual warfare.

Paul refers to our ability to "withstand in the evil day" *(Ephesians 6:14)*. This text does not refer to the judgments of the Great Tribulation after the Rapture of believers worldwide. It is for today.

I believe Satan and demons evaluate every Christian and the advancements the Christian is making for Jesus Christ against their devilish campaigns of darkness. In the devil's conference room believers are profiled and demonic spirits are dispatched against them to mitigate their testimony and effectiveness for Jesus. Paul admitted, "...we wanted to come to you—even I, Paul, time and again—but Satan hindered us" *(2 Thessalonians 2:18)*.

Often unseen, these subtle invasions of demonic attacks on our spouse, our children, grandchildren, and ourselves are the work of demons that are doing everything in their power to destroy us. We know what God's Word has promised:

- "You are of God, little children, and have overcome them, because He who is in you is greater than he who is in the world" *(1 John 4:4)*.

- "He has delivered us from the power of darkness and conveyed us into the kingdom of the Son of His love" *(Colossians 1:13).*

Our spiritual contest against demons is a daily battle, and the level of intensity is proportionate to our effectiveness and fruitfulness for Jesus Christ. That is our routine warfare. Make no mistake: in addition to routine warfare, demons have planned special "evil days" for you. Here is an example.

Assume you are a businessman or woman and you check into a hotel. At the exact time someone of the opposite sex checks in as well. That person makes a pass at you. You are far from home and extraordinary temptation suddenly attempts to convince you to consider adultery. You shake yourself and wonder, How did that scenario get in my mind?

Welcome, to your "evil day."

Here is another scenario: You are endeavouring to minister on behalf of Jesus Christ when suddenly you find yourself in a "holy war" with another believer. Gossip begins, and you suffer slander. It eats at you. Bitterness takes root in your mind and spirit. You develop retaliatory thoughts and before long, they consume you.

Welcome, to your "evil day."

Plan ahead for the "evil days" demonic spirits will add to your calendar so you can withstand them. In those trying and very difficult moments, know how to put on your spiritual armour.

I became a Christian in 1973 and have seen a number of "evil days"—times when I distinctly remember demonic spirits trying to destroy me. Perhaps I was the target of these enemy assaults because thousands of students have come to faith in Jesus Christ through my ministry. In addition, through the years I have written and spoken on themes of youth suicide, the occult, sexual permissiveness, and other topics that have upset demonic spirits because young people responded by the thousands to these truths.

WHY DEMONS ATTACK

I've been in Satan's bull's eye for many years, but I suspect you have too. Now, if you are just a "couch potato" Christian, don't expect much demonic attack. Why should demons bother with you? They've already got you! But you have problems too because you have forgotten that we are to maintain our body—our physical temple of God—with honour and discipline (see 1 Corinthians 3:16).

Christians who don't make gains for Jesus Christ, passive Christians, or Christians who don't pray, are mostly a waste of time for busy demonic spirits.

It's a good sign when demons target a minister, church, or ministry. It means God is using them and they are obeying Jude's command: "And on some have compassion making a distinction; but others save with fear, pulling them out of the fire, hating even the garments defiled by the flesh" *(Jude 22-23)*.

Demons despise when a Christian or church becomes evangelistically focused and creatively shares faith in Christ with the lost. Yet today churches often seem more interested in holding regular business meetings and adding up financial numbers than adding up numbers won to Christ. Instead of reaching out to the lost, many churches have become self-service cafeterias that cater to serving believers. Many a church began their ministry on fire for God and slowly became neutralized by the enemy. A vibrant, Spirit-filled church sharing the message of the Gospel effectively is a juicy target for demonic spirits!

When I first came to Christ I had an overwhelming consciousness of everyone around me who did not know the Lord. I shared about Christ with nearly everyone and everything that moved. Early in our marriage Cristie and I held each other accountable.

"Did you witness to the lady who checked you out at the grocery store?"

"Jerry, did you share Christ with anyone who was on your flight?"

Back then both of us were very soul conscious. Through the years demonic spirits have tried to put out my fire for reaching the lost.

THE PROS AND CONS OF BIBLE STUDY

Did you know there are "cons" to studying the Bible? If we are not aware of the enemy's tactics, we can become so absorbed in Bible study and personal enrichment that we let days, weeks, and months go by without sharing the love of Christ one-on-one with the people God sovereignly leads across our path. Demons will let us have a Bible study if it replaces our evangelistic outreach.

I am not against Bible studies. We need instruction from learned teachers of God's Word to deepen our faith, but we have to guard against becoming so "deep" that we stop sharing our faith with people who don't know Christ.

As a young evangelist I preached for Dr. Adrian Rogers at the great Bellevue Baptist Church, Memphis, Tennessee—a huge church with thousands of people. One day I overheard someone ask Dr. Rogers if he believed in "election"—in God selecting certain people for salvation. The person added, "Only the elect will get to heaven."

"I believe in election," Dr. Rogers responded, "and have learned that the harder I work at evangelism, the more people get elected."

What a great response!

Demons prompt pastors to give eloquent sermons without giving people a chance to receive Christ at the end. What salesman would pitch a product and not ask for the sale? Yet it happens in thousands of churches every Sunday. Fervour for the lost has been lost, because the enemy has dulled compassion in the hearts of believers and turned their vision inward.

The night I came to Christ, June 21, 1973, I was seated in the very back row of the Windermere Youth Camp at Lake-of-the-Ozarks, Montana. I had sat in that back row three nights barely listening to the speaker. This was the last night of camp. Eleven weeks prior I was checked out of St. Luke's Hospital where I had been hospitalized for taking drugs and for depression. If I hadn't come to Christ that night, I wonder if I ever would have.

Do you know how I came to Christ? A beautiful girl named Cindy walked all the way to the back row before the sermon began and said, "Jerry, come sit with me tonight. I want you to hear the message." Because she was so attractive, I decided to go sit with her. God used her invitation to rescue me in the nick of time.

What caused Cindy to care for a lost, visibly confused and dejected kid like me? The love of Jesus Christ in her heart! We have to be very careful when demons tempt us to lose our love for the lost, for fellow believers regardless of their behavior, and for Jesus and His Word.

Our assignment as kingdom citizens is to win the lost, yet Ephesians 2:2 tells us that people who are lost walk "according to the course of this world, according to the prince of the power of the air, the *spirit* who now works in the sons of disobedience." The minute we engage in evangelism, take people out of the grip of this evil spirit and point them to Jesus Christ, we stir up demonic warfare. We must understand how to use our spiritual armour as protection.

OUR SPIRITUAL WARDROBE

We find both our defense and our offense in our spiritual

armour that is modeled on the armour of the Roman soldier. The renowned pastor of Westminster Chapel in London and former medical doctor Martin Lloyd Jones wrote:

> We must bear this in mind as we proceed to the interpretation of the significance of these parts in this whole armour of God. The Apostle Paul as a prisoner was familiar with Roman soldiers and always having to look at them. Chained sometimes to a soldier on the right hand and on the left, it came very naturally to him to use such a comparison and to say, in effect, "This is a picture of what we have too in a spiritual sense."[57]

SIGNIFICANCE OF THE BELT

"Stand therefore, having girded your waist with truth ..." (*Ephesians 6:14a*).

The Roman soldier's belt represents truth. When a person is not committed to personal integrity—to telling the truth—have you noticed the damaging effects on their life and the lives of those around them? Think about it! The effect of the absence of truth on your life, in your employment, in your marriage, and on your children would be cataclysmic. Insights into truth can be gleaned through an understanding of the belt.

1. Preparedness: The Roman soldier always wore a tunic—an outer garment that served as his primary piece of clothing. It was usually made of a large, square piece of material with holes cut out for arms. Ordinarily it draped loosely over most of the soldier's body, but leaving a robe loose was never the custom in battle. Since the greatest part of ancient combat was hand-to-hand, a loose tunic was a potential hindrance and even a danger. Before battle it was carefully cinched and tucked into the heavy leather belt that girded the soldier's loins.

The belt, therefore, was very important to a Roman soldier's wardrobe. It secured his armour. Spiritually the belt represents truth. Truth in our lives is the essential virtue that causes the rest of our armour to be secure and protective. The belt of truth buckled securely around a Christian's waist is a mark of preparedness that indicates the Christian soldier is ready for spiritual truth and is serious about fighting demonic spirits. Any form of deception, exaggeration, or prevarication will cause our spiritual armour to slip and fall off leaving us unprepared for the blows of the enemy.

2. Honesty, strength and confidence: John Stott, who *Christianity Today* referred to as "an architect of 20th century evangelicalism [who] shaped the faith of a generation," wrote, "Usually made of leather, the soldier's belt belonged rather to his underwear than his armour. Yet it was essential. It gathered his tunic together and also his sword. It ensured he was unimpeded when marching. As he buckled it on, it gave him a sense of hidden strength and confidence."[58]

3. Personal integrity: Integrity (truthfulness) will gird us just like the belt girded a Roman soldier.

Truthfulness before God and our fellow man will give us confidence and strength in our spiritual battle. Sin rarely enters our lives when we are honest with God and ourselves, but what if we become aware that we have sinned and haven't been honest with people in the past? The best way to close that door of access to demonic spirits is to confess before the Lord any less than honest actions you may have taken, such as dishonest words you may have spoken, misrepresentations you may have made, or actions where you may need to make restitution to make things right.

For instance, have you lied to your employer? You say no, but if you are not giving your job all the energy and skill you can, in essence you are not being truthful with the job description, which was the criteria by which you were hired.

Are you telling the truth to your wife or husband? Do you tell "white lies?" Be very careful to repent of this kind of behavior because it will allow demonic spirits to gain advantage over you.

Cristie and I are both blessed with earthly fathers who are men of immense personal integrity. There is never anything questionable in their lives. Both our dads have never said to us, We are honest, but never have we questioned their integrity. What an example they have set for us!

4. Knowledge of God's Word: The word "truth" Paul used in our text is ἀλήθεια, and it means "hiding nothing." This word is used various ways in Scripture. In Proverbs 12:17,19, it denotes "that which is opposed to falsehood." In Isaiah 59:14,15, Jeremiah 7:28, it means "fidelity or truthfulness." The doctrine of Christ is called "the truth of the Gospel" *(Galatians 2:5)*, or "the truth" *(2 Timothy 3:7; 4:4)*. Our Lord says of Himself, "I am the way, and the truth" (John 14:6).[59] The content of God's truth is in the Bible, and again, we must know the truth to counter the many lies demons plant in our minds.

5. Attitude of truthfulness: The word "truth" also refers to the attitude of truthfulness. It is the mark of every sincere believer to forsake hypocrisy and any form of sham. In reality, truth guarantees all the other virtues and habits of the believer.

SIGNIFICANCE OF THE BREASTPLATE

Scripture reveals the second piece of defensive armour for the Christian is a breastplate of righteousness: "Stand therefore, having girded your waist with truth, having put on the breastplate of righteousness" *(Ephesians 6:14)*.

The breastplate is essential if we are to be ready for battle. Its meaning is both simple and very profound. How vital it is that you understand it's true, deep meaning!

Two features of the Roman soldier's breastplate speak to the meaning of the breastplate of righteousness:

1. The breastplate provided a soldier protection in battle. MacArthur adds, "No Roman soldier would go into battle without his breastplate, a tough, sleeveless piece of armour that covered his full torso. It was often made of leather or heavy linen, onto which were sewn overlapping slices of animal hooves, or horns, or pieces of metal. Some breastplates were made of large pieces of metal molded or hammered to conform to the body. The purpose of that piece of armour is obvious—to protect ... vital organs." [60]

The breastplate is clearly an important piece/part of armour because of the parts of the body it covers: heart, lungs, stomach, intestines, liver, kidneys, and spleen—all are essential to existence and life. To suffer a wound in these vital organs is fatal.

Charles Hodge was at Princeton University during an era when the Seminary produced hundreds and hundreds of biblically literate, theologically conservative ministers who had great knowledge and skill in preaching. For more than 50 years that dear man was mightily used of God to impact the world through the seminarians he so carefully trained. Hodge reflected on the breastplate: "A warrior without his breastplate was naked, exposed to every thrust of His enemy and even to the random spear. In such a state flight or death is inevitable."

2. The breastplate covered a soldier's front. The scholar Ernest Best points out, "While armour for the back was sometimes provided, none is mentioned here suggesting that if the Christian warrior does not stand firm but turns and runs he is completely vulnerable."[61]

We will examine righteousness in light of the Roman soldier's breastplate. Please understand the tremendous spiritual significance of the breastplate of righteousness. We live in an age when people don't understand the term "righteousness." Several translations of Scripture have unfortunately substituted the words "integrity" and "goodness" for "righteousness," and this is a grave error. The correct term is righteousness, and we must strive to learn its meaning. It is clearly alluded to in the passage we are studying.

Righteouness means "right standing before God." Let me help you understand the depth of this amazing Bible doctrine.

There is a debate in theological circles: Is this breastplate of righteousness the righteousness we receive from Christ when we become Christians, or is it our own personal righteousness as we walk and obey God? Let me give you the answer: it is both! The breastplate symbolizes the believer's righteousness in Christ as well as his righteous life in Jesus Christ:

1. Imputed righteousness: "For He made Him who knew no sin to be sin for us, that we might become the righteousness of God in Him" *(2 Corinthians 5:21).*

The fact that righteousness is imputed forms the whole foundation of our standing as believers in Jesus Christ. An alternative term is justification by faith. Because we can never attain to God's perfect standard of righteousness, God sent His one and only Son into this world that He might through Him give us His righteousness. This type of righteousness is described in several passages of Scripture.

In other words, God took our sins and imputed them to His Son, Jesus Christ. That means, God put our sin on Him, and charged them to His account. That is precisely the meaning of imputation—you take something that belongs to one person and place it into the account of another.

How does this happen?

When I believe and invite God's Son Jesus into my life, God imputes Jesus' righteousness—His perfect observance of the law and obedience to God in me. God adds to my account righteousness. He imputes it to me—the righteousness of His own Son, and He clothes me with it! That's why Peter wrote that after we believe in Christ we become "partakers of the divine nature" *(2 Peter 1:4)*. The Holy Spirit takes up residency in our hearts and quickens our spirit within us. Our spirit is the distinct part of our being that is God-conscious and becomes grieved when we sin and fail the Lord.

2. Imparted righteousness: "And that you put on the new man which is created according to God, in true righteousness and holiness" *(Ephesians 4:24)*.

This text indicates that God does not stop with imputed righteousness. He also works in me the righteousness of His own Son Jesus. In other words, God's righteousness has not only been put on me as a cloak and covering, but God also infuses righteousness in me as I obey, saturate my mind with His Word, and reciprocate to Him in prayer.

Really, imparted righteousness is comparable to a blood transfusion where the blood from one person flows into the blood and circulation of another person. It can be "transfused," "infused," "injected," or "imparted"—these are all terms that refer to the same spiritual transformation and operation that takes place in every person who becomes a new creature in Christ (see 2 Corinthians 5:17) by receiving Jesus as their Saviour.

I have heard scores of testimonies through the years of alcoholics delivered, the addicted set free, the abusive who have become loving, and the depressed who have become filled with hope. It happened to people from all walks of life, every ethnicity, and all ages as they turned to Jesus Christ. The behavioural changes of these redeemed people are irrefutable.

How are you living your life? The way you live either fortifies you against demonic attack, or makes defeat easy. The breastplate of righteousness provides protection from Satan's attacks against us. We must wrap our whole being in righteousness just like the ancient Roman soldiers covered themselves with the breastplate of armour.

It is hard in our day for believers to be aware of how important it is to walk in personal righteousness. Two actions on our part ensure our walk of righteousness. Let's look at two illustrations.

1. Unquestioned obedience: An aviation cadet on a practice flight was suddenly stricken with blindness. Frantic, he contacted the control tower and informed them of his desperate plight. His commanding officer radioed back, "Don't be afraid, just do what I tell you." After advising him to keep circling the airfield until all was cleared for his emergency landing, the officer instructed the cadet to begin descent.

As the aircraft approached the runway, the officer's voice encouraged him, "You're coming in right on target." The cadet gave unquestioned obedience to his officer's every instruction. Had he not given unquestioned obedience to his commanding officer, he would have died.

Unquestioned obedience brought peace and safety in the midst of his personal storm.

Hitler's pastor-prisoner Dietrich Bonhoeffer once wrote, "Only those who obey can believe, and only those who believe can obey."

The lack of obedience is a big problem in our society. Doctors across North America say the second most difficult patients, other than those who do not pay their bills, are the ones who refuse to follow orders. Doctors report that large numbers of patients take only half their medications and leave pill bottles half-full, cheat on their diets, continue to smoke, or never return for checkups in spite of careful prescriptions and cautious advice.

How often do we treat God's instructions the way we do a doctor's prescription? Are we obedient?

2. A listening ear: A missionary who was translating

Scripture into an indigenous language was struggling to find a word for "obedience." One day he called his dog to himself, and the dog came running. A local commented, "Your dog is all ear!" That statement gave the translator the word he needed for obedience—to be "all ear." Are you listening to God on a daily basis? Are you "all ear" to what He is saying?

A HEART FOR GOD

The heart is an organ that weighs about 12 ounces. If the heart beats at 72 beats per minute, it pumps 45 pounds of blood per minute, 2,700 pounds of blood per hour, and 32.4 tons of blood per day. It is a muscle that never rests except between beats.

Every 30 seconds all the blood in the body passes through the heart. It has a grip greater that that of one's fist. The two ventricles of the heart hold an average of ten ounces of blood that is pumped out at each beat.

What a miracle is this little, vital organ! It does one-fifth of the mechanical work of the body and exerts enough energy each hour to lift its own weight 13,000 feet into the air.

Heart disease can end a person's life.

There is an analogy between the physical heart and the spiritual heart. When a person has a "heart for God" they go the extra mile, they are sensitive to the Lord, they hunger for the things of God, and they care for people. Without a heart for God, a "head for God" can't carry out righteousness in a practical way on a daily basis. We can intellectually understand biblical truth without our heart being engaged for the Lord. Remember, Paul said if "I give my body to be burned, but have not love, it profits me nothing" *(I Corinthians 13:3)*. We need to keep our spiritual heart "clean" before the Lord.

How is your spiritual heart? Is it clean, or have you allowed contaminants into your spiritual "blood stream"—that daily flow in your life of practical righteousness as you yield yourself to God and make your body an "instrument of righteousness to God" *(Romans 6:13)*.

Righteousness can't be legislated. In other words, you can't make someone spiritual. When the Lord instructed parents to "train up a child in the way he should go" *(Proverbs 22:6)* it meant for them to instill desire in the child to love the Lord. We instill desire in our children to love the Lord more by what we do than what we say. My kids have heard me preach hundreds of sermons, but I can assure you, they have watched my life much closer than they have listened to my sermons.

My wife, Cristie, and I were blessed by God to have three children: Danielle, Jeremy, and Jenilee. The greatest desire we had for our children was for them to have a heart for God. We knew we couldn't mandate that request, and we knew that legalistic or liberal Christianity would not foster its fulfillment. We prayed often through the years that we would be an example and that we would be honest concerning our own failures and imperfections before our children.

All three of our kids are grown, married, and serving God in great ways. As I reflect back on my years of parenting I distinctly remember when demons tried to lead my children away from God and away from a love for God. Had I not been praying and listening to the Lord, demonic forces would have succeeded. I am convinced Satan had a sinister, carefully designed plan to destroy Danielle, Jeremy, and Jenilee. The demonic attacks they experienced were uniquely different, and yet very real.

Parents have asked me for more than 30 years how to raise children who will love the Lord. My first answer is for parents to have a heart for God. Sin, impurity, and temptations of the flesh and the world kill our hearts for God if we sit idle and don't use the spiritual gifts the Holy Spirit has given us for fruitfulness in God's service.

By studying, learning, and wearing the six essential pieces of armour, both Cristie and I have been graced by the Lord to overcome all the fiery darts and schemes the devil has sent our way. We have lived through demonic oppression and demonic attack, and we know it won't end until we leave this world and enter the kingdom of heaven.

Are you keeping a spiritual covering over your children by the fidelity of your walk with Jesus Christ? Are you protecting your spouse from demonic attack? A praying father covers his children with spiritual protection. A mother interceding daily for her children provides mighty spiritual protection. Do you remember what Jesus said in Matthew 12:28-29? "But if I cast out demons by the Spirit of God, surely the kingdom of God has come upon you. Or how can one enter a strong man's house and plunder his goods, unless he first binds the strong man?"

Demons attack a father in an attempt to attack his children. The enemy assails a mother in his endeavour to bring menace to her children. Praying parents form an umbrella of spiritual protection over their children. It does not negate demonic attack against their children, but it is a strong deterrent.

Paul wrote, "And be found in Him, not having my own righteousness, which is from the law, but that which is through faith in Christ, the righteousness of God by faith" *(Philippians 3:9).* The breastplate of righteousness protects the heart!

RIGHTEOUSNESS IN THE LIFE OF A BELIEVER

Up to this point we have gained many insights into the meaning of both the breastplate and righteousness. Now we will see how these elements work together to shape the life of a believer.

To summarize, the breastplate of righteousness first gives us a general sense of confidence essential to our warfare. Then, as for toddlers, it helps us begin to walk with confidence through experience over time. As we do, we grow in the grace and knowledge of Jesus Christ (see 2 Peter 3:18).

If you engage the enemy in spiritual battle with uncertainty or hesitancy, you are already defeated. Uncertainty occurs when you are unsure whether you are truly a believer, unsure of God's sovereign plan manifested through trials and problems, and illiterate in His Word. Once you understand your right standing (righteousness) in Jesus Christ, you can enter spiritual warfare with the absolute assurance of victory no matter how difficult the warfare. The righteousness of Christ in us gives us confidence.

Too many pastors are guilty of supplying believers with "paper armour" of good advice, seminar sermons, meaningless programs, endless activities, human techniques and methods, when believers are desperate for the godly armour of holy living. No program, method, or technique can bring wholeness and happiness to the believer who is unwilling to confront and forsake sin. MacArthur writes:

> *Many, if not most, of the emotional and relational problems Christians experience by a lack of personal holiness. Many of our disappointments do not come from circumstances or from other people, but from our own unconfessed and uncleansed sin. And when circumstances and other people manage to rob us of happiness, it is because we are unprotected by the armour of a holy life. In either case, the cause for our unhappiness is our own sin. David committed adultery with Bathsheba and ordered the death of her husband, Uriah, and he had no peace. That is why the great Psalm of penitence or those sins includes the plea 'restore to me the joy of Thy salvation' (Psalm 51:12). Unholy living does not rob us of our salvation, but it robs us of salvation's joy.*[62]

When I receive imputed and imparted righteousness from Jesus Christ, there is righteousness in my own life. It is that simple. Demons tremble at Christians who are filled with the Holy Spirit, walk in the Spirit, and look at every event in their life through the lens of faith and obedience to Jesus Christ.

Technically, New Testament usage of "righteousness," *dikaiosync*, refers to our justification before God as well as to the moral quality of the Christ-likeness in our lives. John Calvin, the great Geneva theologian, saw righteousness as uprightness of character and loyalty in principle and action to God. Someone has said, "When a man is clothed in practical righteousness, he is impregnable. Words are no defense against accusation, but a good life is!"

Isaiah portrayed God as a warrior, righteousness being one of His attributes. Paul, a Jew, was familiar with these Scriptures as he studied the Roman soldier to whom he was chained.

- "Righteousness shall be the belt of His waist, and faithfulness the belt of His loins" *(Isaiah 11:5)*.

- "For He put on righteousness as a breastplate, and a helmet of salvation on His head; He put on the garments of vengeance for clothing, and was clad with zeal as a cloak" *(Isaiah 59:17)*.

Thus we see that God's righteousness followed by our personal obedience is more than adequate to protect our spiritual heart from all demonic attack. John Phillips notes:

The genius of the Gospel is that God does not ask us to imitate His righteousness, for no human being could possibly do that. Instead God gives us His Holy Spirit to live within us and to reproduce Christ's righteousness of God to the world. The world is waiting to see men and women behaving like Jesus.[63]

Well said!

One of the devil's key strategies is to play on our feelings. I have learned never to trust my feelings. One minute you are up, and one minute you are down. Nowhere in the Bible is there the admonition to put our trust in our feelings. Your feelings will deceive you. Instead, we anchor all of our emotions to the promises in God's Word.

Scripture is objective; feelings are subjective. The subjective must always follow the objective. When you put the subjective before the objective, you will always be confused. The breastplate gives you the confidence to say: Here I stand, a "soldier" in Christ, and I know something about the enemy. I have examined his dispositions, I have discovered something about the powers he commands and the armaments he uses, and I know they are characterized by subtlety, power and strength. I am also aware of the sensitive organs within me that are exposed to his attack. Until I have confidence that they are covered and protected (until I am convinced my breastplate of righteousness is fastened securely), I cannot possibly stand and be ready for the battle that continually assails me if Jesus wants to use me to glorify God through my life. The moment I put on the breastplate of righteousness, I know all is well and I am ready.

I undergird my righteousness through obedience daily by "Casting down arguments and every high thing that exalts itself against the knowledge of God, bringing every thought into captivity to the obedience of Christ" *(2 Corinthians 10:5)*.

To put on the breastplate of righteousness is to live in daily, moment-by-moment obedience to God. This part of God's armour speaks of holy living. God supplies the standard and power, but I provide the daily willingness. God Himself dresses me with imputed righteousness in Christ, but I put on practical righteousness.

Homer wrote that light-armed warriors, those who did not wear a breastplate but armed themselves with linen corselets, could not stand. Why? The breastplate provided protection from "fiery darts."

Paul refers to fiery darts the enemy aims at our mind, body, and spirit. In ancient warfare fiery darts were arrows dipped in pitch, or some other combustible material that was set on fire before being launched at the enemy. These darts not only wounded, but also burned. Fiery darts were aimed and thrown with the intent to kill or disable. They were among the most dangerous weapons used in ancient combat.

Paul wrote, "Above all, taking the shield of faith with which you will be able to quench all the fiery darts of the wicked one" *(Ephesians 6:16).*

We know when a demon's "fiery dart" has penetrated our armour, don't we? It renders us prayerless and weak toward sin. We have a sense that we're on our own. We may attempt to lean on our own understanding. What a mistake! We quickly become confused. Our mind fills with worry, and anxiety grips our body as if we were in a vice.

Demons shoot fiery darts at our mind to get us to question God and His plan for our life. Often they fire these darts when we are in the midst of great trial or spiritual testing. Again, we must not trust our feelings—they will betray us. We must raise the shield of faith and make certain our breastplate is firm and secure with the imputed righteousness of Christ coupled with our personal righteousness.

Anders adds, "The breastplate of righteousness pictures the metal armour in the shape of a human torso common to the Roman uniform. To put on the breastplate can be understood as choosing not to harbour and nurture known sin. It is striving to be like Christ and live according to His ways of righteousness."[64]

Pray and ask the Lord if you have allowed any disobedience

in your life. Reflect and meditate before God. Take time to allow the Lord to speak to your heart and spirit. Remember:

- "For this is the love of God, that we keep His commandments. And His commandments are not burdensome" *(1 John 5:3)*.

- "Now he who keeps His commandments abides in Him, and He in him. And by this we know that He abides in us, by the Spirit whom He has given us" *(1 John 3:24)*.

- "And if anyone does not obey our word in this epistle, note that person and do not keep company with him, that he may be ashamed" *(2 Thessalonians 3:14)*.

George Muller, a man whose breastplate of righteousness was firm and secure, was born into a German tax collector's family. Early in his life, George learned to steal, gamble and drink. As a teenager he stayed in expensive hotels and snuck out without paying the bill. Finally he was caught and jailed. Prison did Muller little good. Upon release he continued his crime spree until one fateful Saturday night in 1825 when he was led to faith in Jesus Christ.

In obedience to God, Muller developed a deep prayer life. He carefully recorded his prayer requests and the answers that came from the Lord. Each answer to prayer was a stunning story of God's faithfulness to His own.

During the course of Muller's 93 years of life, he housed more than 10,000 orphans, "prayed in" millions of dollars for God's work, traveled to scores of countries preaching Christ, and recorded 50,000 answers to prayer.

You cannot imagine the blessings God has for you if you will simply obey Him. Now let's study another vital piece of spiritual armour.

DISCUSSION QUESTIONS

1. Name some ways a tsunami is similar to an attack of the enemy.

2. Why do demonic attacks come? Have you been subject to demonic attack for any of these reasons?

3. What are some ways that demons attack the local church? What types of attack has your church faced?

4. Is it possible to study the Bible too much? Describe a situation when Bible study can be a hindrance to a life of faith.

5. The belt was part of the Roman soldier's armour. Name three ways this piece of armour applies to our walk with the Lord.

6. What is the difference between imputed and imparted righteousness?

7. What two important actions do you have to take to undergird your walk of righteousness?

CHAPTER 10

THE FIERY DARTS
OF DEMONS

"A bove all, taking the shield of faith with which you will be able to quench all the fiery darts of the wicked one" *(Ephesians 6:16).*

I am amazed how many churches, ministries, and pastors believe that when things are going well and there is no agitating trouble, it is an indication of God's blessing. Without being judgmental, let me simply say that demons do not bother ministers or ministries that are not changing people's lives, or having an impact on culture with the power of the Gospel. Sadly, this is why some clergy and churches do not identify with any thought of spiritual warfare, let alone the devil and demons.

The first century Church changed the culture of its day. Christians were mighty change agents in the Roman Empire. Do you remember the accusation brought against Jason and his fellow believers? It was said "these who have turned the world upside down" *(Acts 17:6).*

We are living in a day when the World is changing the Church.

Theodore Epp founded the great radio ministry, *Back to the Bible,* based in Lincoln, Nebraska. Epp was a godly minister who had great spiritual and biblical insight. One day he realized something was wrong because he stopped receiving critical mail.

Convinced that he was not challenging the people enough, he changed his preaching and remarked, "I am afraid that when I'm pleasing with everybody, I am not pleasing the Lord, and pleasing the Lord is what counts."[65]

John Wesley, who God used to rock England in a mighty spiritual revival, asked the young men he had sent out to preach two questions: "Has anyone been converted?" and "Did anyone get mad?" If the answer was "No," Wesley told them he did not think the Lord had called them to preach the Gospel, and dismissed them. [66]

When Charles Spurgeon, pastor of London's Metropolitan Tabernacle, sent his ministerial students to pastor churches, he gave them this charge, "Cling tightly with both your hands—when you fall, catch hold with your teeth; and if they give way, hang on by your eyelashes!" [67]

If you are doing anything for God, you are going to experience demonic attack. If you do not have any spiritual warfare in your life, be careful, that is not a good sign! As long as you are sitting on the shelf and not be used of God, demons will leave you alone. But watch what happens when you start sharing your faith in Christ with lost friends and spending time in prayer and Bible study daily. Demons will be dispatched to trip you up. Expect it!

Nearly 400 years ago a ship of travelers landed on the northeast coast of America. You may know the story—the first year they established a town site; the next year they elected a town government; the third year the town government planned to build a road five miles westward into the wilderness. The fourth year the people tried to impeach their town government because they thought it was a waste of public funds to build a road fives miles westward into a wilderness.

Who needed to go there anyway?

These were people who had had the vision to cross the

Atlantic, had seen themselves enduring a 3,000-mile journey and overcoming great hardship to accomplish it, but just a few years later had not had enough vision to see five miles out of town. These pilgrims had lost their pioneering vision.

With a clear vision a church or believer will find no ocean too great to cross. Without vision we rarely see beyond our current boundaries.

Jesus prayed for you and me, "I do not pray that You should take them out of the world, but that You should keep them from the evil one" *(John 17:15).*

Jesus confronted the religious leaders of His day, "You are of your father the devil, and the desires of your father you want to do. He was a murderer from the beginning, and does not stand in the truth, because there is no truth in him. When he speaks a lie, he speaks from his own resources, for he is a liar and the father of it" *(John 8:44).*

John discerned, "We know that we are of God, and the whole world lies under the sway of the wicked one" *(1 John 5:19).*

Spurgeon wrote, "Satan's house has a front chamber full of everything that is enticing to the eye and bewitching to the sensual taste; but there is a back chamber, and no one knoweth, no one hath seen the whole of its horrors." [67]

I have seen the horrors of what demons can lead people to do. We filmed an eye-opening documentary coast-to-coast about the way our sexualized culture is destroying our youth. Included in this video were segments about the illicit sexual behavior of kids in grade seven or eight and the subsequent devastating consequences.

In no other area have I seen demonic handiwork manifest more effectively than in youth suicide. In my previous book, *Why They Die: Curing the Death Wish in Our Kids*, I provided story after story of young people who took their lives. Behind every suicide is the murderer, Satan.

Christians leaders are cautioned, "Moreover he must have a good testimony among those who are outside (the faith), lest he fall in reproach and the snare of the devil" *(1 Timothy 3:7)*.

Spurgeon notes again, "He (Satan) is more cunning than the wisest, how soon he entangled Solomon! He is stronger than the strongest, how he fatally overthrew Samson! Ay, and men after God's own heart, like David, have been led into most grievous sins by his seductions." [(68)]

HOW DEMONS AFFLICT BELIEVERS

- "And the Lord said, 'Simon, Simon! Indeed, Satan has asked for you, that he may sift you as wheat. But I have prayed for you, that your faith should not fail; and when you have returned to Me, strengthen your brethren" *(Luke 22:31-32)*.

- "Therefore submit to God. Resist the devil and he will flee from you" *(James 4:7)*.

Let's look at some ways demons afflict the believer.

1. By the permission of God for a specific godly purpose. We see this example in Job: "So Satan answered the Lord and said, 'Does Job fear God for nothing? Have You not made a hedge around him, around his household, and around all that he has on every side? You have blessed the work of his hands, and his possessions have increased in the land. But now, stretch out Your hand and touch all that he has, and he will surely curse You to Your face!' And the Lord said to Satan, 'Behold, all that he has is in your power; only do not lay a hand on his person'" *(Job 1:9-12)*.

Clearly, we see that God designed a purpose for allowing Satan to have access to Job and his family. For centuries Job has served as the quintessential example that godly people often suffer for a godly purpose. I have been comforted many times by reading the book of Job and considering the severe trials that Job endured. His trials make my trials seem so small. But notice the agent of his trials—it is the devil! Here we see the sovereign power of Almighty God.

2. By yielding to sin and temptation. We can commit "gateway" sins whereby demons can enter our lives. Sexual sins, the abuse of drugs or alcohol, pornography, idolatry, the occult, and self-indulgence are just a few we can name. "Then, when desire has conceived, it gives birth to sin; and sin, when it is full-grown, brings forth death" *(James 1:15)*.

FIERY DARTS OF THE WICKED ONE

"Above all, taking the shield of faith with which you will be able to quench all the fiery darts of the wicked one" *(Ephesians 6:16)*.

The language of combat and warfare is not in vogue in much of the preaching today, and there have been eccentricities of teaching on demon warfare that have added to the silence on the topic by some clergy. However, we must remember there are many places in the New Testament where the Christian life is presented in just these terms:

- warfare (see 2 Corinthians 10:4; 1 Timothy 1:18)

- conflict (see Philippians 1:30)

- striving (see Colossians 1:29; Hebrews 12:4)

- a great struggle (see Hebrews 10:32)

- a race (see 1 Corinthians 9:24)

- discipline (see I Corinthians 9:27)

- a conflict between good and evil (see Romans 7:21)

- life and death (see Romans 6:13, 23).

In this warfare we are participants, not just spectators. We are dependent on the power of Christ if we are to survive it.

Peter says in his first letter we are not to be surprised at the "fiery trial" that tests us as if something strange were happening to us (see 1 Peter 4:12; I Corinthians 10:13). God tests us "that He might know all" *(2 Chronicles 32:31)* that is in our hearts.

Warren Wiersbe tells the story about how he and an older, wise pastor-friend went to hear a young preacher who had great acclaim and promise. As the young man preached so eloquently, Wiersbe leaned over and whispered into the ear of the older pastor next to him and asked, "What do you think ... isn't he great?"

The sage responded, "He has not suffered enough yet."

We do not know what we are made of until we suffer and enter into spiritual conflict. Anyone can say the right words about faith and Christianity when everything is going well, but wait till the deep trials hit you! Evaluate your commitment to Jesus Christ in those moments.

Watch someone close to you become ill or die.

Experience a person telling lies about you and impugning your character.

Let tears roll down your cheeks as you see your son or daughter make disastrous decisions with their lives.

In moments such as these we truly discover who we are and what our faith is made of. In addition, during these trials, tests, and temptations of life demons come to attack you as severely as possible to eliminate your passion and love for the Lord.

One early Church leader referred to the harrowing days of spiritual warfare in our lives as "the dark night of the soul."

Hosea experienced this dark night of the soul. He watched with a broken heart as his wife became a prostitute. How embarrassing this must have been to the prophet of God. In my mind I can see Hosea, with tears streaming down his face, preaching and saying to the people of his day, God loves you in spite of your spiritual adultery just as I love my wife who has left me for the pleasures of other men.

God tested Hosea, and through Hosea's deep grief demonstrated to Israel His own unending love for the Israelites in spite of their sin. I have always loved Hosea 11:4: "I drew them with gentle cords, with bands of love, and I was to them as those who take the yoke from their neck. I stooped and fed them."

The Bible records, "When the Lord began to speak by Hosea, the Lord said to him: 'Go, take yourself a wife of harlotry and children of harlotry, for the land has committed great harlotry by departing from the Lord'" *(Hosea 1:2)*.

When his wife finally repented and came back to God and her husband, she came home with a child from another man. Hosea revealed God's unconditional love toward her, embraced her, and loved that illegitimate child as if it were his own.

May I encourage you with this thought as you enter into spiritual warfare? God will use the spiritual combat we experience to reveal His strength to us in new and powerful ways. Job's struggle with Satan concluded with a defeat that is an amazing victory. Initially reduced to silence by all the trials, Job finally manages to reply directly to God: "I have heard You by the hearing of the ear, but now my eye sees You" *(Job 42:5)*.

ON GUARD AGAINST FIERY DARTS

"Above all, taking the shield of faith with which you will be able to quench all the fiery darts of the wicked one" *(Ephesians 6:16)*.

Where do fiery darts hit? John Phillips said:

Paul had often seen the shields of Roman soldiers carried into war. The shields were made so that a row of soldiers could lock shield to shield, forming a wall of iron. Such a wall would be difficult, if not impossible, for a foe to penetrate. Each individual shield was big enough to cover the whole soldiers' body. Darts and arrows hurled at the soldier hit the shield and fell harmlessly to the ground. The wicked one throws many darts. [69]

As we progress in faith, we are subjected to demonic assaults similar to what the character in John Bunyan's allegory *Pilgrim's Progress* experienced. His name was Christian. Demonic spirits hurled fiery darts at him to try to stop his spiritual growth. Again—we can expect it too! It shouldn't surprise us, but we should recognize it as a good sign, not a bad one.

Harold Ockenga had a keen mind concerning spiritual warfare. He said:

The ancient Roman soldier had a large, oblong piece of wood or metal covered with hides which he used to turn off arrows tipped with some burning substance. I suppose that these fiery arrows were as terrible to the men of antiquity as the flame-throwing tank is to the soldier of today. With this shield the soldier could ward off burning arrows and even quench them. Faith is such a shield for the Christian." [70]

Scripture identifies areas where we are susceptible to demonic attack and fiery darts from the evil one. We need to be on guard regarding these areas.

In my 30-plus years of ministry I have observed some of the most prominent destinations that fiery darts of the wicked one target in people.

1. The lusts of the flesh: engagement in illicit sexual behavior, abuse of drugs and alcohol, and involvement in pornography which is now transmitted digitally to every device imaginable. The Bible say, however: "Do not love the world or the things in the world. If anyone loves the world, the love of the Father is not in him. For all that is in the world—the lust of the flesh, the lust of the eyes, and the pride of life—is not of the Father but is of the world" *(1 John 2:15-16)*.

Every Christian needs an accountability partner—someone with whom they can be real and honest about what's going on in their life. Husbands need to be honest with their wives about any form of temptation that comes into their lives, and vice versa.

My wife Cristie and I often do a spiritual check-up on each other. We share our spiritual strengths, but we also share our spiritual weaknesses. We pray transparently together for each other and include the specific areas where we could get tripped up by the fiery darts of the wicked one.

Through the years the enemy has shot many darts at us. Only through prayer and abject honesty with each other have we been graced by God to hold the shield of faith against these attacks.

I have applied another accountability measure to my life. My son Jeremy can log into my computer at any time through Log-me-in. Jeremy can review what is on my computer and provide spiritual accountability for me.

Our flesh is weak and prone to sin. We can minimize the enemy's attack against us through spiritual safeguards and sincere honesty with people close to us. Set up safeguards in your life.

The Evangelical with perhaps the greatest national standing in the 1930's was G. Campbell Morgan, the minister of Westminster Chapel. When he heard Martyn Lloyd-Jones preach in 1938, he wanted to have him as his associate and successor. Jones' education was at Saint Bartholomew's Hospital, better known simply as Bart's. Bart's carried the same prestige in the medical community that Oxford did in the intellectual community.

Martyn's career was in medicine. He had succeeded in his exams at such a young age that he had to wait to take his MD. At that time he was already chief clinical assistant to Sir Thomas Horder, one of the best and most famous doctors of the day. Soon it became apparent that God was calling Martyn Lloyd-Jones to preach, and as a result the world was never the same.

G. Campbell Morgan was an Armenian and his Bible exposition, though famous, did not deal in the great doctrines of the Reformation. Martyn Lloyd-Jones was of the tradition of Spurgeon, Whitefield, the Puritans and the Reformers, yet the two men respected each other's positions and talents, and their brief partnership—until Campbell Morgan died at the end of the war—was peaceful and furthered the work of Christ in London.

As the storm clouds of World War II gathered, Morgan was set for retirement. Martyn Lloyd-Jones assumed the full pastorate of Westminster Chapel. The ensuing years were a time of extreme trial for everyone in London. Its citizens endured month upon unending month of night raids by Hitler's bombers. At one point early in the war there were 57 successive nights of bombing. Winston Churchill wrote of that period, "At this time we saw no end but the demolition of the whole Metropolis."

Since Westminster Chapel stood in close proximity to Buckingham Palace and other important government buildings, it was in constant peril of being utterly destroyed. The church fellowship experienced a continual state of financial and emotional crisis.

After the war the congregation grew quickly. In 1947 the church balconies were opened, and from 1948 to 1968 when Jones retired (after 30 years of pastoring), the congregation averaged 1500 on Sunday mornings and 2000 on Sunday nights.

During the summer of 1947 the doctor made a visit to the

United States and was received warmly. At the request of Carl
F. H. Henry, he spoke at Wheaton College. The five sermons he
delivered were published as *Truth Unchanged, Unchanging.*
In them Lloyd-Jones set forth his belief concerning the kind of
preaching the world needs.

He claimed that a strong character and a strong leader
cannot avoid controversy. He was opposed to arbitrary unions
between denominations based on pragmatism rather than
doctrine. Nothing caused more trouble for Martyn Lloyd-
Jones than his unswerving and unpopular belief in the need to
adhere to certain foundational doctrines. The doctor opposed
the marriage of biblical preaching and secular psychology.
He believed that even in a secular age people respond to the
uncompromised truth—a view that was confirmed as liberal
churches emptied and evangelical ones maintained their cause.

One day, Martyn received a visit from Pastor Chuck Smith of
Calvary Church, Costa Mesa, California, who told him that his
books had transformed Smith's own preaching. Pastor Chuck
confessed that he had driven himself into mental breakdown in
an attempt to use his personality to communicate his sermons.
Since that time he had let the Bible speak for itself, and as a result
both his ministry and his own health had benefited enormously.
He didn't tell Jones that his Sunday morning congregation was
running at 24,000 in attendance.

Pastor Chuck founded the Calvary Chapel movement in
1965, and today it thrives with more than 1,400 churches
worldwide. The constant within this movement has been that of
pastors who preach expository sermons using the entire Bible.

Jones wrote an extensive commentary on Ephesians
6:10-18—the armour of the believer. The following is a brief
quote regarding fiery darts:

*In addition to all his other activities, and all the
implements or the instruments he employs, the*

*devil employs these fiery darts. And they are fiery;
they burst into flame and are very destructive. An
understanding of this is of vital importance to us in our
spiritual warfare. Many masters of the spiritual life
have described these attacks in detail. The best known
examples are Martin Luther and John Bunyan.*[71]

As great a Christian as the Apostle Paul was, he reminds us
in his letter to the Church at Rome of the constant conflict he
experienced with lusts of the flesh. If Paul experienced such a
great inward struggle, we will too: "For I know that in me (that
is, in my flesh) nothing good dwells; for to will is present with
me, but how to perform what is good I do not find. For the good
that I to do, I do not; but the evil I will not to do, that I practice.
Now if I do what I will not to do, it is no longer I who do it, but
sin that dwells in me" *(Romans 7:18-20)*.

2. Mental attacks: thoughts of doubt, fear, anxiety, stress
and hopelessness. Nowhere do demons work more diligently
than in their attack on our mind.

We have already studied the tremendous battle for the
mind and our defense of saturating it with Scripture. Nothing
can replace daily Bible reading, meditation, and Scripture
memorization.

In addition, we must be wise in what we allow our minds to
feast on.

The Christians at Philippi were chronic worriers. Paul
addressed their anxiety and admonished them: "Be anxious
for nothing, but in everything by prayer and supplication, with
thanksgiving, let your requests be made known to God; and the
peace of God, which surpasses all understanding, will guard
your hearts and minds through Christ Jesus" *(Philippians
4:7-8)*.

Our solution is to live in a constant attitude of prayer
"without ceasing" *(1 Thessalonians 5:18)*. Every need or issue

of our lives must be brought to God in prayer immediately and continually. Paul revealed the result of a prayerful mind and heart:

- "Finally, brethren, whatever things are true, whatever things are noble, whatever things are just, whatever things are pure, whatever things are lovely, whatever things are of good report, if there is any virtue and if there is anything praiseworthy—meditate on these things. Those things which you learned and received and heard and saw in me, these do, and the God of peace will be with you" (*Philippians 4:8-9*).

- "Let this mind be in you which was also in Christ Jesus" (*Philippians 2:5*).

Jones gives us the clue to the source of idiotic and evil thoughts that hit our mind:

"But what of our experiences? Do we not all know something of this? Do we not know something of what it is, perhaps, to wake up in the morning and to find that before we have had time to do any thinking, thoughts come to us, evil thoughts, perhaps even blasphemous thoughts? You were not thinking, you were doing nothing, you had just awakened; but suddenly the darts reach you. That is what the Apostle means by 'the fiery darts of the wicked one.'"[72]

3. Doubt—mistrusting God: The Christian life, as we will examine in the next chapter, is a life of faith. We must put our total trust and confidence in the Lord regarding every situation and life experience. Spurgeon used to say, "When you cannot trace God's hand, you can always trust God's heart."

Puzzling things happen to believers. The Lord has permitted some of the best Christians I have known to die what seemed a premature death. But Paul said we see physical events as if in a mirror dimly (see I Corinthians 13:12). On this side of heaven, therefore, I cannot possibly understand why God allows certain things to happen. I must place my entire trust and confidence in a God who controls everything.

Habakkuk, the prophet, was overwhelmed with the question, "Why, God?" The Lord had raised up the evil nation of Babylon to destroy His own people due to their sin and disobedience. In the midst of this dismal reality God told Habbakkuk to proclaim His message to Israel. It was a seemingly impossible assignment. Like us, when we pray and nothing seems to change the situation, Habukkuk cried out: "O Lord, how long shall I cry, and You will not hear? Even cry out to You, 'Violence!' and You will not save'" *(Habakkuk 1:2)*.

I have said the same thing to God in prayer concerning anguishing situations in my life. When I look at the moral deterioration of Canada and the United States I can become overwhelmed. I ask, "How can we change this, Lord? Why are you allowing this to happen?"

Then, I remember God is working in ways I can't see. For example, I have never seen a righteous saint suffer and die without God using their passing to bring people to faith in Jesus Christ. The suffering of the Lord's people has broken some of the hardest hearts.

God chooses certain believers for extreme trials and even death to build His kingdom. Through our brokenness other people are often brought to fullness in Jesus Christ. Habukkuk eventually conceded to the secret of allowing God to do His work even when he didn't understand: "Behold the proud, His soul is not upright in him; but the just shall live by his faith" *(Habakkuk 2:4)*.

Some day we will know. Some day we will understand. But now we must take every experience in life by faith. We must put our full trust and confidence in the Lord. Retrospectively, we can never point to a time when God has failed us.

Let go, and let God work in your life! Obey him in those dark moments. He will come through for you in His time. He came through for Joseph in an Egyptian prison. It took 13 years of confinement for Joseph to understand why all the bad things had happened in his life. God had had a plan.

Paul's repeated imprisonment produced what we refer to as the "Prison Epistles"—Ephesians (where we learn the profound truths of the armour of the believer), Philippians (a treatise, interestingly, on joy), Colossians (some of the greatest Christology of the New Testament), and Philemon. Think of the millions of believers through the centuries who have been blessed and instructed by these texts Paul wrote during the many days of his incarceration in the loneliness of a jail cell! These Scripture verses stand true:

- "Trust in the Lord with all your heart, and lean not on your own understanding; in all your ways acknowledge Him, and He shall direct your paths" *(Proverbs 3:5-6)*.

- "Jesus said to him, 'If you can believe, all things are possible to him who believes.' Immediately the father of the child cried out and said with tears, 'Lord, I believe; help my unbelief'" *(Mark 9:23-24)*.

Listen to the words of Dr. Martyn Lloyd Jones:

Have you not found that, when you have been engaged in prayer or are trying to pray, these darts come from all directions at you? When your one desire is to be concentrating on God and on worship and prayer and adoration, you seem filled with all these distracting, and perhaps evil thoughts and notions and ideas.... You can read a newspaper and concentrate on it, but when you start reading the Bible, thoughts and ideas come from all directions and you find it almost impossible to concentrate. Where do they come from? These are 'fiery darts of the wicked one.' [73]

4. Physical attack by God's permission: We can open ourselves to demonic attack physically through personal disobedience to God. In these cases he may grant the enemy permission to attack us. This is a curious area of Scripture, and we do not know all the reasons.

At times the Lord allows fiery darts to inflict physical pain on us. This type of attack is different from the type of demonic attack we have studied to this point. We know that in cases of demonization, we can see physical self-harm. Also, we have learned that demonization always sources itself in a habitual sin practiced by a person. Such demonization is not uncommon.

But we observe in the life of Paul, the great Apostle, and Job, a righteous man, that God allowed fiery darts to cause a kind of inexplicable physical attack. In each case there was a divine reason, and the result was a greater dependency on the Lord. Some of us need to walk, like Jacob, with a limp of dependency on the Lord. If we didn't have areas where we have to be completely dependent on the Lord, arrogance and pride might lead us to believe in ourselves and cause us to fall flat on our faces. God kept Paul humble in his sheer dependency on the Lord because of a physical ailment:

And lest I should be exalted above measure by the abundance of the revelations, a thorn in the flesh was given to me, a messenger of Satan to buffet me, lest I should be exalted above measure. Concerning this thing I pleaded with the Lord three times that it might depart from me. And He said to me, 'My grace is sufficient for you, for My strength is made perfect in weakness.' Therefore most gladly I will rather boast in my infirmities, that the power of Christ may rest upon me (2 Corinthians 12:7-9).

Clearly, the Lord allowed this "buffeting" to keep Paul humble and dependent. Phillips observes:

Satan has a thousand wiles and he will never give up. If you successfully resist him now, he will come again later. Perhaps he will tempt you with something in a book or on television, a clever remark by a college professor, or a friend's snub or sneer. Perhaps he will arouse a sleeping lust or put an utterly lewd or corrupt thought in your mind. We will never be out of range of Satan's fiery darts, but they can be quenched and rendered harmless by the shield of faith.[74]

5. Division—designed to keep Christians in disunity and disharmony. Did you know there are more than 41,000 Christian denominations in North America? That's a staggering thought! Many of them had a wonderful beginning and continue with the blessing of God. But sadly, some of these denominations were started due to disunity and disharmony. There are enough Christians in our world to evangelize the population inhabiting the globe. What hinders the universal Church of Jesus Christ from fulfilling the Great Commission?

Disunity and division among the family of faith is top of the list. Satan knows the power of the Church of Jesus Christ united in the cause of evangelism and he counteracts it with disunity. Churches and ministries are plagued with gossipy members second-guessing the ministry and what is going on. These believers are effective at dividing the body of Christ and will be responsible to the Lord someday. Watch out for those fiery darts of gossip, dissension, and a desire to hear bad news about one of the Lord's followers!

Let's look at a scriptural example.

The Corinthian Church decided to divide themselves by their favorite spiritual teachers and leaders. Paul rebuked the division and wrote:

> *Now I plead with you, brethren, by the name of our Lord Jesus Christ, that you all speak the same thing, and that there be no divisions among you, but that you be perfectly joined together in the same mind and in the same judgment. For it has been declared to me concerning you, by those of Chloe's household, that there are contentions among you. Now I say this, that each of you says, "I am of Paul," or "I am of Apollos," or "I am of Cephas," or "I am of Christ." Is Christ divided? Was Paul crucified for you? Or were you baptized in the name of Paul?* (I Corinthians 1:10-13).

Did you notice Paul pointedly stated that Chloe's house had given him this report? He did not say, Somebody told me.

Be very careful about believers who quote "somebody" and don't disclose the source of the information. That is called gossip, and it has hindered and destroyed thousands of weak believers and churches. I am convinced disunity is Satan's number one strategy to keep the Church of Jesus Christ from world evangelization.

Spurgeon cautioned of this demonic attack:

> *It is a sickening thought, that while Christians frequently quarrel, we never hear of the devils doing so. The Church of God is divided, but the kingdom of darkness appears to be one. Whatever internal strife there may be between evil spirits, we have no hint of it here; they all seem to act in complete unison. Whether hate is a more compacting principle than love, I will not venture to say; but certainly these haters of God*

and His truth appear to be knit together as though they were one devil rather than a multitude of evil spirits, yet the lovers of Jesus Christ are not knit together as one man under His blessed rule.[75]

We live in a world where character assassination has become a sport and garners ratings in the media. Protect the reputation of the Lord's people! Hold up your shield of faith when a fellow believer wants to gossip about another Christian. Tell them, Let's go minister to the person you are talking about. You can stop a gossip cold in their tracks when you remind them of one of the seven abominations of the Lord: "A false witness who speaks lies, and one who sows discord among the brethren" *(Proverbs 6:19).*

We have to investigate three more pieces of armour that prepare us for spiritual combat: spiritual shoes, the shield of faith, and the helmet of salvation. You will be encouraged when you understand their purpose. Let's examine them very closely in the next chapter.

DISCUSSION QUESTIONS

1. Name some of the great preachers in history who welcomed dissention. What can we glean from the unusual stand they took?

2. Explain two ways demonic spirits can attack a believer.

3. The Christian life can be expressed in terms of combat and warfare. On your own, or in a group, write out and/ or read the applicable Scripture verses. Consider to what degree they apply to your life.

4. Have you experienced a "dark night of the soul"? Reflect on, or share some of your experiences. Were they orchestrated by the enemy?

5. What is the importance of an "accountability partner"? If you don't already have one, consider who you would approach to fill this role for you.

6. Under what circumstances might God allow the enemy to afflict us with pain physically?

7. How do disunity and division begin? What is their effect?

CHAPTER 11

————+————

SHOES, SHIELD OF FAITH, HELMET OF SALVATION

"**A**nd having shod your feet with the preparation of the Gospel of peace; above all, taking the shield of faith with which you will be able to quench all the fiery darts of the wicked one. And take the helmet of salvation..." *(Ephesians 6:15-17a).*

YOUR SPIRITUAL SHOES

"And your feet shod with the preparation of the Gospel of peace" *(Ephesians 6:15).*

Solid footing is essential when you are engaged in hand-to-hand combat. To slip and fall could mean sudden death. The Roman soldier wore sandals with hobnails in the soles to give him better footing in battle.

If we are going to "stand" and "withstand," then we need the shoes of the Gospel. Because we have peace with God (see Romans 5:1) that comes from the Gospel, we need not fear the attack of Satan or men.

Too many Christians do not know how to stand for truth. Demons hurl fiery darts of doubt into their minds, and when challenged with questions about their faith, or the claims of Christianity, they are unable to answer cogently.

If our "Gospel of peace" shoes are not firmly on, we will slip and fall as we engage in spiritual warfare. You have to be able to stand for the Gospel before you have the capacity to spread the Gospel.

The most widely known Bible verse among adult and teen believers, according to Barna Research, is "God helps those who help themselves." This "verse," however, is *not* found in the Bible and actually conflicts with the basic meaning of Scripture. This is one example of the proliferating biblical illiteracy of our age. There are many other examples that challenge us with the question, Is the spiritual depth level of our contemporary sermons adequately equipping believers with the doctrinal knowledge they need?

Less than one out of every ten believers possesses a biblical worldview as the basis for his or her decision-making behavior. A biblical worldview occurs with an understanding that the Bible synthesizes truth through a presentation of clear absolutes, a view of God's holiness and all His other immutable attributes, and gives us spiritual principles by which to live. When given 13 basic teachings from the Bible, only one percent of adult believers firmly embraced all 13 as being biblical perspectives. (76)

Gary Burge, Ph.D., professor of New Testament at Wheaton College, Wheaton, Illinois, asserts that biblical illiteracy is at a crisis level not just in our culture in general, but in America's churches: "If it is true that biblical illiteracy is commonplace in secular culture at large, there is ample evidence that points to similar trends in our churches."(77) Burge's interaction with Wheaton New Testament students revealed:

- fully 80 percent could not place Moses, David, Solomon, and Abraham in chronological order;

- half the students could not sequence the following: Moses in Egypt, Isaac's birth, Saul's death, and Judah's exile;

- one-third could not identify Matthew as an apostle from a list of New Testament names;

- when asked to locate the biblical book supplying a given story, one-third could not find Paul's travels in Acts, half did not know that the Christmas story was in Matthew, half did not know that the Passover was in Exodus.[78]

This leads us to wonder what is being taught and preached in evangelical churches today. Are pastors delivering warmed over sermons from *Reader's Digest*? Are Sunday school teachers using the Bible at all? Does Sunday school even still exist?

If you don't *know* anything, you cannot *stand* for anything. Like Professor Burge, George Lindbeck, the famous Yale University theologian has commented on the decreasing knowledge of Scripture. "When I first arrived at Yale, even those who came from nonreligious backgrounds knew the Bible better than most of those now that come from churchgoing families."[79]

Author and theologian David Wells has the same opinion. He says, "I have watched with growing disbelief as the evangelical church has cheerfully plunged into astounding theological illiteracy."[80]

A scientific survey called PISA (Program for International Student Assessment) tested the knowledge of people in 32 industrialized countries. The results of the study reveal an "insidious biblical illiteracy" even in Christian circles, says Volker Gaeckie, dean of students at Albrecht Center in Tubingen. "Christians should heed PISA's warning that text comprehension is a problem."[81]

One hundred and fifty freshmen in a Christian college were selected because they grew up going to church and were active members in evangelical churches. These students were given a biblical knowledge test. The answers to the questions were disturbing to say the least. Here is a sample of the answers these church-reared students provided:

- the history of Abraham was found in the book of Ruth;

- the Roman persecution was the greatest event in the Old Testament;

- the Exodus was the return of the Jews to Palestine after World War II;

- the Ten Commandments were given by Jesus on the Mount of Olives; and some of the Wisdom books of the Old Testament are: Acts, Paradise Lost, and The Lord of the Flies;

- Genesis was the first Gospel;

- the mother-in-law of Ruth was Mary Magdalene and her famous great-grandson was Noah;

- Jesus was baptized in the Red Sea, was betrayed by Samson, and died in Bethlehem.[82]

If the moral deterioration of our culture were not so catastrophic, these test results would be laughable. Our young people are being defeated in spiritual warfare because they do not know the Bible, its promises, its power, and its illuminating effect on every decision needed in life. "My people are destroyed for lack of knowledge" *(Hosea 4:6).*

Mark Twain said, "A classic is a book which people praise and don't read." That statement, unfortunately, applies to the Bible in our contemporary culture. It is the most widely distributed book (2.5 billion copies) and the least read. We must change this statistic if we are to be victorious against the demonic spirits arrayed against us.

The preaching of pastors in our churches has changed progressively from the days of the early forefathers of our faith.

History records that Puritan preachers were "the first American intellectuals." In colonial America sermons typically foreswore personal narratives and commonplace illustrations in favour of biblical exegesis and doctrinal exposition. Parishioners, in those early days, received from the pulpit a thorough education in theology from the Bible—something woefully lacking today.

Read the books of Stephen Prothero, professor in the Department of Religion at Boston University and the author of numerous books on religion in America. He is one of my favourite authors. Prothero's research reveals that the sermons of these early pastors of the republic were typically "doctrinal lectures" such as a person might hear in a theological classroom.

In our shallow entertainment age, sermons have become more therapeutic and less instructional and theological, and the validity of what we do on Sunday morning too often is grounded in what we feel, not in what we think and learn. Bible passages are taken out of context by contemporary ministers who search for stories that evoke an emotional response, or a desired attitude. As a result, the heart of a "good sermon" is fast becoming the "emotional work" that can be done in 20 minutes of preaching time.

Sermons contain therapy and not theology, happiness rather than salvation, story-telling instead of Bible doctrine, and arousal of emotions instead of stimulation of the intellect.

Our faith is emotional, but it is to be more than emotion.

Many Christians accept elements of these unbiblical worldviews without even knowing it. Because of this, George Barna and Mark Hatch have noted, "...we cannot really call the faith of American Christians a Bible-based faith. It is a synthetic, syncretic faith." According to Barna and Hatch, Christians today have accepted and integrated so many ideas from other worldviews and religions that they have created their own faith system.

"The average born-again, baptized, church-going person has embraced elements of Buddhism, Hinduism, Judaism, Islam, Mormonism, Scientology, Unitarianism and Christian Science without any idea they have just created their own faith."[83]

Pollster George Gallup commented that Americans revere the Bible, but they don't read it. And, because they do not read the Bible, they have become a nation of "biblical illiterates." Mark Twain also said that the Bible is the most popular book nobody has read.

How can a generation be biblically educated in its understanding of human sexuality when it believes Sodom and Gomorrah to be a married couple? Christians who lack Bible knowledge are the products of churches that marginalize biblical knowledge. Bible teaching often accounts for a small fraction of the typical church's time and attention.

Prothero reminds us that the United States is one of the most religious places on earth, but it is also a nation of shocking religious illiteracy. Prothero makes the stunning case that to remedy this problem we should return to teaching religion in the public schools.

Let me explain Prothero's reasoning. English professors surveyed at major American colleges and universities see knowledge of the Bible as a deeply important part of a good education. In fact, 100 percent of university professors surveyed by the *Bible Literacy Project* stated, "Students need to know the Bible in order to be well educated."[84]

Virtually all (98 percent) of high school English teachers reported the same, explaining that kids were "clueless, stumped, and confused" and did not know enough about the Bible to properly understand British and American literature, as well as art, music, history, and culture.

In 1963, the Supreme Court ruled that public schools may not require devotional use of the Bible. In that same decision, however, the Supreme Court explicitly acknowledged that academic study of the Bible in public schools is constitutional as part of a good education. Academic study of the Bible in public schools is therefore legal in all 50 states of the union.

In his majority opinion to the court in *Abington v. Schempp*, Justice Thomas Clark wrote: "It might well be said that one's education is not complete without a study of... the history of religion and its relationship to the advancement of civilization. ...Nothing we have said here indicates that such study of the Bible, or of religion, when presented objectively as part of a secular program of education, may not be effected consistently with the First Amendment." [85]

Teachers in the study cited a wide range of literature that contains biblical allusions, such as *The Grapes of Wrath, Animal Farm, Great Expectations, The Sound and The Fury, To Kill a Mockingbird, Song of Solomon, Brave New World, Romeo and Juliet, Hamlet, The Pearl, A Separate Peace,* and *Lord of the Flies*, to name only a few.

The following are a few teachers' remarks on the relevance of the Bible to the study of English literature:

- "It's difficult to pick up a work of literature that doesn't have some reference to the Bible."

- "I think all the more complex works of literature reference it."

- "I wouldn't say [literature] is steeped with it. It's saturated with it."

Once upon a time, Americans were a people of the book. They knew what it said. They carried with them on their New World pilgrimages not only a thirst for adventure but also Psalters, New Testaments, and Bibles which they read, memorized, cited and recited, searched for more meaning and quoted with authority. Colonists used this literacy first and foremost to read the Bible, which throughout American history has been both the bestselling book and most influential cultural artifact.[86]

Ironically, the church of modern times stands for very little. Truth is reduced to subjective thinking. Preferences replace convictions.

The first century believers of the Christian Church did not die as martyrs because they were wishy-washy. To deny that Caesar was God meant certain death. As a young Christian I read *Foxes Book of Martyrs*, which chronicles the stories of hundreds of believers who met excruciating torture and death during the first few centuries of Christianity because they stood unwaveringly for the truth of the Gospel.

To wage a successful battle, your spiritual shoes must be on at all times. You must know *what* you believe and *why* you believe it. The truth we proclaim in Jesus is based, not upon our own opinions, but on the authoritative Word of God. The shoes Paul refers to are a believer's stability, or surefootedness in the Gospel that gives him peace so he can stand in the battle.

The Roman soldier could use his short sword effectively to cut and kill his enemy because he had traction. How can you have "traction" in your spiritual engagement with demonic powers if your mind is not filled daily with reading and studying the Bible?

Warren Wiersbe comments on the shoes of the Gospel:

> But the shoes have another meaning. We must be prepared each day to share the Gospel of peace with a lost world. The most victorious Christian is a witnessing Christian. If we wear the shoes of the Gospel, then we have the "beautiful feet" mentioned in Isaiah 52:7 and Romans 10:15. Satan has declared war, but you and I are ambassadors of peace (2 Corinthians 5:18–21); and, as such, we take the Gospel of peace wherever we go. [87]

Prothero points to six cooperating causes of biblical literacy in colonial America:

1. The home: In the colonies and in the early republic, Bible instruction and reading took place first and foremost in the home. In fact, in 1642 the Massachusetts Bay Colony passed legislation that required families to teach their children "to read and understand principles of religion."[88]

We know what has happened to the home in Canada and the United States: divorce rates have skyrocketed to nearly 50 percent; the greatest growth now is among couples living together outside of marriage, and the media assault on traditional family unit is tragic.

2. The church: Puritan sermons were arranged in a four-part scheme of Bible text, doctrine, reasons, and uses. In Virginia in 1631 a law required each minister to "examine, catechize, and instruct youth and ignorant persons of his parish in the Ten Commandments, the Articles of Belief, and the Lord's Prayer. New England ministers took the duty to transmit basic religious literacy to the next generation.[89]

3. Schools: The first textbook in the United States public school was the Bible! Children learned their ABC's from Scripture-saturated textbooks, or the Bible itself. Historian Jennifer Monaghan states that early literacy education amounted in essence to "a course in Christianity."[90]

Our school grounds have regrettably become battlegrounds. Columbine has repeated itself in cities across North America where students have gunned down classmates and teachers. The Newtown, Connecticut massacre claimed the lives of 26 people, 20 of them children shot dead in their elementary classroom by Adam Lanza. Someone has said that we cannot hand out Bibles in public schools, but we can distribute condoms.

4. Sunday school: The Sunday school movement migrated from England to the United States in 1790. The United

States model focused on teaching "the leading doctrines of the Bible."[91] Sunday school, however, is quickly becoming a relic of the past. Small groups now utilized by many churches are tremendous for fellowship and friendship, yet many complain that the teaching quotient is shallow.

5. Bible and tract societies: In the past missionaries working on the western frontier needed the Word of God in print, and Bible and Tract Societies were born. The American Bible Society founded in 1816, plus many more, banded together and produced Bibles and tracts of all shapes and sizes. Although still active, the influence of the Bible societies is almost nil.

6. Colleges: America's first three colleges, Harvard (1636), William and Mary (1693), and Yale (1701) were founded to train ministers of the Gospel to teach God's Word. At Harvard, where the vast majority of the library's books were works in divinity, faculty taught students to "know God and Jesus Christ," and also to understand Jesus as "the only foundation of all sound knowledge and learning."[92]

At least five of these six institutions (home, church, schools, Sunday school, Bible/Tract societies and colleges) have come under ferocious demonic attack. Sadly, the Ivy League colleges have left their mandate to train ministers with the Holy Scriptures far behind. In fact, most Americans and Canadians are not even aware these colleges began with a godly purpose. The theology departments of these particular colleges have changed dramatically. Their secularization, loss of a biblical worldview, and dramatic moral changes clearly illustrate the transition.

If demons can keep Christians illiterate, Christians cannot use their "sword of Spirit" offensively to ward off the evil minions Satan dispatches. We can remember in the garden of Eden, the serpent quizzed Eve, "Has God really said?" Today this question is echoed in the citadels of higher learning that once adhered to the authoritative truth of the Bible. The person of God is questioned, the moral absolutes of Scripture have been rejected, and the *theory* of evolution is taught as empirical fact. I am not certain a creationist or scientist who embraces intelligent design can get hired in the science departments of these Colleges as alleged in Ben Stein's movie *Expelled: No Intelligence Allowed* (2008). Theological departments remain, yet Scripture is not studied as the inspired Word of God. Instead, demons inspire ideas that morph into cults, which have become increasingly popular in our generation because we have left our biblical moorings.

Every day when you get out of bed, the first thing you must do is to put on your spiritual shoes. Be ready to "stand" grounded on your knowledge of God's truth and unchanging character. Remember God's promise: "For He Himself has said, 'I will never leave you nor forsake you.'" The Greek scholar Kenneth Wuest helps us understand the potency of this biblical passage in the original Greek:

> The word 'leave' is not the usual word which means 'to leave,' leipo (λειπο), but aniemi (ἀνιεμι) 'to send back, to relax, to loosen, not to uphold, to let sink.' It is preceded by two negatives in the Greek text, which in English make a positive, but which in Greek only serve to strengthen the negation. It is 'I will not, I will not cease to sustain and uphold thee.' The word 'forsake' is a compound of three Greek words, egkataleipo, eg (ἐγκαταλειπο, ἐγ) meaning 'in,' kata (κατα) meaning 'down,' and leipo (λειπο) meaning 'to leave.' Leipo (Λειπο) has the idea of forsaking one, kata (κατα) suggests rejection, defeat, helplessness, and eg (ἐγ) refers to some place or circumstance in which a person may find himself helpless, forsaken. The meaning of the word is that of forsaking someone in a state of defeat or

helplessness in the midst of hostile circumstances."[93]

If you put your spiritual shoes on and stand, the Lord will stand right there at your side helping you fight every spiritual battle that comes your way. Again, remember, the key to standing is knowing the truths of the Bible. Open your Bible and get in it every single day!

When those fiery darts of the wicked one come your way, raise your shield of faith in Jesus' name. Take your sword of the Spirit, which is the specific Word God has given you about whatever situation demons may be throwing at you, and watch them flee!

THE SHIELD OF FAITH

"Above all, taking the shield of faith with which you will be able to quench all the fiery darts of the wicked one" *(Ephesians 6:16).*

We battle demonic forces only by faith. Notice the metaphor Paul uses to illustrate the faith a believer requires in spiritual combat. He uses a shield, and not just any kind of shield. The Williams translation reads, "Besides all these, take on the shield which faith provides, for with it you will be able to put out all the fire-tipped arrows shot by the evil one" *(Ephesians 6:16).*

As mentioned before, this was a very specific shield. Vincent explains:

'The shield of faith' (τὸν θυρεὸν τῆς πίστεως). Θυρεόν shield, is from θύρα door, because [it was] shaped like a door. Homer uses the word for that which is placed in front of the doorway. Thus of the stone placed by Polyphemus in front of his cave ("Odyssey," ix., 240). The shield here described is that of the heavy infantry; a large, oblong shield, four by two and a half feet, and sometimes curved on the inner side. Sculptured

representations may be seen on Trajan's column. [94]

The Liberty Commentary helps: "The fire-tipped darts are the arrows dipped in combustible material and set on fire in Satan's malignant efforts to destroy you. The shield will quench every one of them without exception. It will stop the missiles and put out the fire."[95]

Wuest adds, "This shield which the Christian soldier uses is faith—a present faith in the Lord Jesus for victory over sin and the hosts of the devil."[96]

Keener further explains, "Before battles in which flaming arrows might be fired, the leather would be wetted to quench any fiery darts launched against them. After Roman legionaries closed ranks, the front row holding shields forward and those behind them holding shields above them, they were virtually invulnerable to any attack from flaming arrows."[97]

The Roman soldier had two kinds of shields: the small round one used for hand-to-hand combat at close range, and the large, oblong shield designed to cover the soldier's entire body. Take particular note of this: the shield of faith covers all the other pieces of spiritual armour:

- belt of truth

- breastplate of righteousness

- shoes

- helmet of salvation, and even

- sword of the Spirit/the Word of God.

Patzia helps us understand:

According to ancient historians, the large, door-shaped protective shield was composed of two layers of wood covered with a flame-resistant hide. The flaming arrows that the enemy shot would strike the shield and burn out without penetrating it. Faith, claims the author, acts like an impregnable shield and will extinguish all the flaming arrows of the evil one. Faith is complete confidence and reliance upon God to give the victory.[(98)]

You may be asking, *What is faith?*

The Bible answers, "Now faith is the substance of things hoped for, the evidence of things not seen" *(Hebrews 11:1)*. It is essential that we have faith in God for the warfare before us. "But without faith it is impossible to please Him, for he who comes to God must believe that He is, and that He is a rewarder of those who diligently seek Him" *(Hebrews 11:6)*.

Spurgeon wrote, "Faith laughs at that which fear weeps over. We are not to look to what we have. The witnesses of the senses only confuse those who would walk by faith. Fret and worry, hurry and haste, are all slain by the hand of faith."[(99)]

Remember, you can't increase your faith by daydreaming and thinking, I need more faith. How does faith come? "So then faith comes by hearing, and hearing by the Word of God" *(Romans 10:17)*.

As we study God's Word, memorize and meditate on Scripture, our faith becomes strong and we use our sword of the Spirit, God's Word, on a moment's notice quite effectively. Someone anonymously wrote, "Little faith will bring your soul to heaven, but great faith will bring heaven to your soul." How true!

After the great missionary William Carey was well established in his pioneering mission work in India, his supporters in England sent a printer to assist him. Soon the two men were turning out portions of the Bible for distribution. Carey had spent many years learning the Indian language so he could produce the Scriptures in the local dialect. He had also prepared dictionaries and grammar guides for his successors to use.

One day while Carey was away, a fire broke out and completely destroyed the building, the presses, many Bibles, and the precious manuscripts, dictionaries and grammar guides. When Carey returned and was told of the tragic loss, he showed no sign of despair or impatience. Instead, he knelt down and thanked God that he still had the strength to do the work over again. He immediately started the whole project from the beginning, not wasting a moment in self-pity. Before his death, William Carey had duplicated and even improved on his earlier translation achievements. That is faith in action!

THE HELMET OF SALVATION

"And take the helmet of salvation" *(Ephesians 6:17a).*

There is no question that this Scripture refers to, perhaps, the area of greatest combat of all—the mind. That's where we face our demonic foes and their suggestions.

God has put within each of us a brain. The brain is an amazingly complex marvel weighing only three pounds, yet containing billions of cells capable of performing an incredibly enormous workload of generating, receiving, and transmitting energy.

Scientists estimate that in 70 years of activity a brain may contain nearly 15 trillion pieces of information. Thousands upon thousands of thoughts can pass through our brain every day, and the brain never tires.

The brain is also capable of some strange things. For example, it permits a person to experience phantom pain where an amputated limb once was.

You are going to face intense demonic attack on your mind. Demons want to invade your thinking and plant thoughts of doubt, fear, anxiety, mistrust, lust, and discouragement in your mind. I meet too may people who are limited by fear from bad past experiences. Fear leaves them with no self-confidence, and the limitation finds its origin in the way they think. How do you think? What feelings are in your mind?

The pollster George Gallup has documented that religious beliefs decline as education levels rise. One of Gallup's charts indicates that 51 percent of Americans with no college education believe in angels and devils, but only 35 percent of college graduates do. Gallup also asserts that belief in the Judgment Day decreases with education.

Futurist writer Douglas Coupland, who dubbed today's young adults, "Generation X," wrote *Life After God*, a poignant book representing a grieving for the first generation raised without religion.

Gen Xers were born shortly before, during, or after the general introduction of digital technologies like Apple's personal computer, or Microsoft's operating system. Both companies were founded in the 1970s. The first personal computers came out in the 1970s when today's oldest Gen Xers came of age. By interacting with digital technology from an early age, Gen Xers have a greater understanding of its concepts.

Theologian William Willmon of Duke University said that Coupland's book offers a glimpse of what it is like to have raised the first generation that stopped believing in God. By the time Generation X became adults, there was nothing left to believe in.

In October 9, 2012, the Pew Research Center released a study, *"Nones" on the Rise.* This study takes a closer look at the 46 million people who answered "None" to the religion question in 2012. According to Pew, one-fifth of American adults have no religious affiliation—a growing trend for years. Perhaps most striking is that one-third of Americans under 30 have no religious affiliation. When comparing this with previous generations under 30, there's a new wrinkle, says Greg Smith, a senior researcher at Pew. "Young people today are not only more religiously unaffiliated than their elders; they are also more religiously unaffiliated than previous generations of young people ever have been as far back as we can tell," Smith told NPR *Morning Edition* co-host David Greene. "This really is something new."[(100)] One in five American adults, and one-third of adults under 30, have no religious affiliation in the United States.[(101)]

Religious and moral taboos once dominant in North America have largely vanished. Sexual permissiveness among middle and elementary school students, an adolescent suicide epidemic in North America, the deterioration of the nuclear family, and the barrage of immoral media again illustrate the indoctrination and change rapidly taking place. Hitler proved that if you can indoctrinate the way young people think, you can change their behaviour. It is obvious that how we live reflects how we think. This is why the social engineers of our day want not just to change minds, but to indoctrinate the children and youth of our day.

This indoctrination constitutes a powerful weapon of spiritual warfare against our minds, but in Ephesians 6:17, Paul states that a Christian thinks differently; his or her mind is protected during spiritual warfare by salvation: "For as he thinks in his heart, so is he" *(Proverbs 22:6),* the wise Solomon wrote centuries ago. What we allow into our mind determines what we are and what we shall become. No wonder John Milton wrote, "The mind is its own place, and in itself can make a heaven of hell, and a hell of heaven." Here are three insights into the way we think:

- Adolf Hitler said, "What luck for rulers that men do not think."

- The late Norman Vincent Peale encouraged us, "Change

your thoughts and you can change your world."

- Cicero wrote, "The diseases of the mind are more destructive than those of the body."

Your thinking affects you and everyone around you. Clear-minded, grounded thinking can save your life and someone else's. Peter gives the instruction, "Therefore gird up the loins of your mind, be sober, and rest your hope fully upon the grace that is to be brought to you at the revelation of Jesus Christ" *(1 Peter 1:13)*.

The New Living Translation reads, "So think clearly and exercise self control. Look forward to the gracious salvation that will come to you when Jesus Christ is revealed to the world" *(1 Peter 1:13, NLT)*.

In Greek, the literal wording is "gird up the loins of your mind." Peter is saying, Let nothing hinder your mind as you put it to work. The picture is clear when we think of a first-century man who tucked the folds of his long, flowing garment under his belt so that he would no longer be hindered in his walk or work. Peter applies that imagery to the mind. For the Christian mind to be effective, all hindrances of worry, fear, and inadequacies must be removed so the believer can serve the Lord.

This is why it is essential for a person to receive Jesus Christ as their personal Lord and Saviour. The minute we receive Christ we become new creatures in Christ Jesus. We have a new capacity to think because of the Holy Spirit who is now residing within us. Our thought-life can come under the control of the Holy Spirit.

Salvation in Jesus Christ is just the beginning. As a believer we must take our worry, anxiety, fear, and stress and give it to the Lord. This does not happen once-for-all at salvation. It requires a daily communion with the Lord. We are to cast all our care, as Peter wrote, on the One who cares for us daily. We do our best and leave the rest to God.

- "Therefore, if anyone is in Christ, he is a new creation; old things have passed away; behold, all things have become new" *(2 Corinthians 5:17).*

- "And do not be conformed to this world, but be transformed by the renewing of your mind, that you may prove what is that good and acceptable and perfect will of God" *(Romans 12:2).*

My wife found she was unable to wage spiritual warfare successfully as a teenager. Cristie desired to please God, but somehow the Christian life didn't work for her. One night when we were dating I explained to her that a person must repent of sin when they come to Jesus Christ in saving faith. "Jerry, I don't think I have ever repented of my sins," was her unforgettable reply that November evening in 1978. "You're kidding, right?" I asked, incredulous. Although she attended church regularly and saw herself as a Christian, she had never been born again. Cristie burst into tears and exclaimed, "Jerry, tell me how to repent and receive Jesus."

We knelt next to one another, and after years of attending church, praying prayers, listening to her dad read Scripture at family devotions, Cristie turned from sin to Jesus Christ for His rich, full, free salvation. Many times since then she has said to me, "If only someone would have told me sooner how to find Christ as my Saviour!"

Indeed, you can go to hell from a church pew just as easily as from a greasy downtown street.

Cristie found freedom in Jesus Christ. She discovered Jesus as a personal Saviour and friend. God immediately gave her a desire to read and love His Word. She reexamined her future vocation and decided to follow Christ in full-time ministry and teaching. Instead of just auditing church sermons, Cristie began to grow in her faith to become an effective teacher of God's Word.

Salvation changes the way we think. Using the analogy of the Roman soldier's helmet, Paul gives us insight into why that happens.

The Roman soldier was required to wear a helmet in battle. It protected his head from injury, particularly from the dangerous broadsword commonly used in warfare during that day. The helmet was tough—made of bronze or iron. It had protective cheek pieces, a visor to protect the face and a lining inside of felt or sponge that made its weight bearable. It was usually decorated with a figure and adorned with a horsehair crest.

This physical helmet protected a Roman soldier's head. Similarly, the spiritual helmet protects the believer's mind and represents a new mind in Jesus Christ. Without a new mind, or new thinking, the Christian life does not work. That's why the Christian life has eluded so many. Those who profess Christianity without possessing salvation are not wearing a spiritual helmet. A door remains open in their lives for demonic forces to hurl fiery darts at their minds and they are led astray with unbelief, doubt, and mistrust in God.

It would have been unthinkable for a Roman soldier to go into battle in full armour without a helmet. With an unprotected head he would have been killed immediately. Enter many "casualty Christians"—people who, without having donned a helmet of salvation, make excuses for why they have left the Church and the Christian faith.

Ephesians 6:17 commands, "And take the helmet of salvation." It sounds so casual in the English translation, yet in Greek the command appears in the imperative mood in the place of a participle. It means "take," or "receive" (*dechomai*). The implication is that you *have* to take or receive it to win. You *must* have the helmet of salvation on! John Phillips tells us how essential this helmet is:

> *We must always remember that the mind is Satan's domain. He goes after the mind to influence our thoughts, words, and deeds. Because our minds are vulnerable, they must be protected by God's salvation. The more we wear the helmet of salvation, the more we will think about the things of God, fill our minds and memories with God's Word, and dwell on His enormous cost of our salvation and its ramifications in our lives. Therefore, the more we wear the helmet, the more we will be protected against Satan's lures and lies.* [102]

The helmet of salvation protects the mind, the citadel of intelligence, from false teaching and gives us confidence and boldness in battle. When you become a Christian you replace old man-centred thinking patterns with God's divine thoughts from His Word. In simple terms, when you become a true believer in Christ, you will start thinking right.

DISCUSSION QUESTIONS

1. Biblical illiteracy is of crisis proportions in the contemporary Church. What evidence have researchers discovered to support this statement? What evidence do you see around you that affirms or counters research findings?

2. What is the main cause of biblical illiteracy in the Church?

3. Describe six causes of biblical literacy in colonial America.

4. In what way does the Roman soldier's shield provide a good illustration of the function of faith in a believer's life?

5. What effect will donning a helmet of salvation have on a person's life? Why?

CHAPTER 12

PRAYING ALWAYS

"**P**raying always with all prayer and supplication in the Spirit, being watchful to this end with all perseverance and supplication for all the saints" *(Ephesians 6:18).*

After I came to faith in Jesus Christ, my Aunt Sara boarded me in her home, employed me in her flower shop, and carefully disciplined me in my newfound Christian faith. She hung flat rose boxes on the wall of her shop with a Scripture written on each, and my assignment was to memorize the Bible verse(s). It took me three days to commit to memory my very first verse: "I have been crucified with Christ; it is no longer I who live, but Christ lives in me; and the life which I now live in the flesh I live by faith in the Son of God, who loved me and gave Himself for me" *(Galatians 2:20).*

By the time my Aunt had finished months of training me, I had memorized more than 1,000 verses of Scripture. Aunt Sara instilled into my heart a love for God's Word. She nurtured in me a desire to take the challenge and memorize entire books of the Bible, primarily Paul's epistles. One Sunday night at church Harold Myers stood and quoted an entire chapter of 1 Peter. I was stunned. "How did he do that?" I asked my Aunt.

"Jerry," she said, "when you love God, you are going to love His Word."

That was all I needed. I purchased a New Testament from The Ark Christian bookstore and during my high school years began to memorize all of Paul's epistles. When I went out on a date with Cristie I asked her to hold my New Testament and check me as I quoted entire chapters of the Bible to her.

Scripture shaped me. Scripture protected me. Scripture kept me clean in my high school years while I grew in faith and started preaching as an Evangelist-at-Large for Youth for Christ.

My Aunt also taught me another unforgettable and valuable lesson that summer of 1973.

We worked at Sara's Flowers all day long, and then we did the deliveries. Often, we would not return to her house on 42nd Street until well after dinnertime. I was always so hungry! She made dinner and we ate and talked about the Lord. After dinner we went to the red carpet in her living room where she would lay prostrate before God on her face and say, "Now, Jerry, let's pray."

I had never seen anyone pray like that. She prayed such long prayers, with repeated tears, as she lifted person after person, need after need, to God in what sounded like a very respectful, yet very intimate conversation. I would peak over at her as she was praying, rather uncomfortable in that new awkward position. She stayed facedown, prostrate before God.

Then it was my turn to pray. I stuttered and stumbled as I articulated my inferior prayer to God, I could hear her whisper, "Yes, Lord! Yes, Lord!" throughout my entire prayer. I had never heard anyone do that. Night after night, my Aunt and I would lay prostrate before God as she taught me how to pray by her example.

Betty King drove me home from school while I attended grade nine at a private academy. Ms. King was an older, mature Christian lady and she always reserved the front passenger seat for me. Several other kids filled the back seat, and I was always dropped off first. What I'm about to share may sound strange to you, but let me share it anyway.

My Aunt had so drilled into my head the importance of

prayer that I told Mrs. King I could not talk on the way home—I had to pray. I would lay my head back on the head rest, close my eyes, and pray all the way home, confessing sin and wanting to be close to the Lord. When the other kids wanted to stop for an ice cream cone I would ask Ms. King to drop me off first. I wanted to race upstairs to my bedroom closet and spend more time in prayer.

The Lord had rescued me from almost committing suicide as a teen. He alone lifted my deep depression on the night of June 21, 1973, when I gave my life to Jesus Christ. It seemed as if God had unlocked the hatch of a hellhole in which I had lived and almost died. Indescribable happiness replaced the emptiness when Jesus came into my life.

When I came to Christ, my dad John, my mom Joyce, and my four brothers Johnny, Jay, Jeff, and Joel were not Christians. I rarely joined them to watch TV. I spent most of my high school years in my Big D, the nickname I'd given my bedroom, reading Christian books and biographies, and writing sermons. I was a fanatic! And, looking back, I am so glad I was. During the years from grades nine to 12, my entire ministry developed with Youth for Christ. It emerged from my walk with the Lord.

Prayer shaped me; prayer protected me; prayer kept me clean. My Aunt had given me an invaluable gift when she disciplined me as a new believer.

Prayer will shape, protect and preserve every believer. Paul underscored the importance of prayer in the instructions he left us (see Ephesians 6). After he presents the six pieces of armor of the believer, what does he say? Four times he repeats in a single verse (see Ephesians 6:18), "You have to pray!"

Make sure you let this verse sink in! The armor, without prayer, is inadequate to give us victory in the demonic attack we face. You cannot win at spiritual warfare without prayer.

A prayerless Christian is a powerless Christian. Prayer gives you spiritual energy to raise the shield of faith. Prayer gives you strength to swing your sword, God's Word, at demonic foes that tempt and try you. Prayer gives you stability to not waffle.

I love Greek scholar Kenneth Wuest's treatment of Ephesians 6:18. Look at it closely:

> 'Always' is en panti kairōi (ἐν παντι καιρωι), 'on every occasion'; the Revision gives, 'at all seasons,' praying at all seasons with every proseuchē (προσευχη) (prayer in general) and deēseōs (δεησεως) (special supplication) in the sphere of the Spirit (that is, directed and empowered by the Spirit). Expositors says: 'This great requirement of standing ready for the combat can be made good only when prayer, constant, earnest, spiritual prayer is added to the careful equipment with all the parts of the panoply.' 'Watching' is agrupneō (ἀγρυπνεω), 'to be sleepless, keep awake.' It means 'to be attentive, vigilant.' It is the opposite of listlessness, expressing alertness. 'Perseverance' is proskartereō (προσκαρτερεω), 'to give constant attention to a thing, to give unremitting care to a thing.'[103]

Too often, we are playing at prayer. One survey reveals the average Christian prays only five minutes a day. That won't get the job done! Five minutes a day will not give you fortitude to fight a spiritual war. If you are only praying five minutes a day, you are fighting spiritual battles in your own strength. Spiritual battles can't be fought with carnal weapons. Many pastors and Christians have entered into this warfare relying on the resources of self, only to find defeat. Look how many men and women have fallen! The spiritual battleground is littered with innumerable, talented, gifted, winsome believers who have depended on the flesh and have been mortally wounded.

A GREAT PRAYER WARRIOR

One of the great personalities to shape Protestantism was

Martin Luther. We sometimes have the impression that the only thing this brilliant monk did was to nail a list of protests to the Wittenberg church door. Nothing could be further from the truth. He worked under God's inspiration, preaching, lecturing, and writing daily. The complete edition of his papers contains thousands of pages. He worked inconceivably hard, and yet in spite of it, Luther managed to pray for an hour or two every day. He said he had to pray because he had so much to accomplish. Prayer gave Luther spiritual power, and power to achieve.

We need that kind of power as well. There is much for us to accomplish in our corrupt and needy world, and we too must pray. Prayer will do the same for us as it did for Luther.

Have you ever read, *A Soldier's Prayer*? It is a thought-provoking poem written by an anonymous Confederate soldier:

I asked God for strength, that I might achieve,
I was made weak, that I might learn humbly to obey.
I asked for health, that I might do great things,
I was given infirmity, that I might do better things.
I asked for riches, that I might be happy,
I was given poverty, that I might be wise.
I asked for power, that I might have the praise of men,
I was given weakness, that I might feel the need of
God.
I asked for all things, that I might enjoy life,
I was given life, that I might enjoy all things.
I got nothing that I asked for, but everything
I had hoped for.
Almost despite myself, my unspoken prayers were
answered.
I am among all men, most richly blessed.

Paul, in one critical verse so essential to spiritual conflict, delineates the components of warfare prayer. Please take particular note of them:

1. "Praying always" *(Ephesians 6:18a):* "Always" designates an unceasing attitude of prayer, particularly when our "evil days" come. When demonic spirits are leading your children astray, be sure you stay in continual prayer. You can pray while you are driving a car, at work, laying in bed at night, and by all means, in a quiet hour reserved for the Lord alone.

"In everything give thanks for this is the will of God in Christ Jesus concerning you" *(1 Thessalonians 5:17).*

Here are some points for staying in continuous prayer.

- Begin your intercession with thanksgiving to the Lord in the midst of the warfare you are experiencing. In doing so, you acknowledge God's sovereign power and control. Candidly, I grew the most spiritually when the battle was most intense.

- Keep giving thanks! Substitute a praising heart for a complaining spirit. Pray in this manner: Lord, you are Master of all demonic spirits. Guide me to put on all my spiritual armor. Alert me to the various cloaked methods of the evil one. Give me a discerning spirit, in Jesus' Name.

- Stay in God's presence. I often pray under my breath, inaudibly, when I am in certain meetings where I need God's wisdom, or when I could be become angry or impatient with petty minded people.

Stay in a constant attitude of prayer. A surprise attack has defeated more than one believer who forgets to "pray without ceasing."

2. "Praying with all prayer and supplication" *(Ephesians 6:18b):* Both prayer and praise change things, but did you know different kinds of prayer are necessary in different spiritual warfare situations? You'd better believe it! Whether you use prayers of supplication, intercession, or thanksgiving (see Philippians 4:6; 1 Timothy 2:1) makes a difference.

For example, prayers of thanksgiving are a great weapon for gaining victory over a demonic attack. "Be anxious for nothing [don't worry about the demonic attack that comes your way], but in everything by prayer and supplication, with thanksgiving, let your requests be made known to God" *(Philippians 4:6).*

Intercession is when we pray for someone other than ourselves. With respect to intercession, Wuest explains, if we examine the original Greek ("prayer" meaning general requests; petition/supplication), Paul is instructing us to pray and "intercede" in the midst of spiritual warfare.

You may wonder how we can focus on someone else when we are in the midst of a spiritual battle. We do it in obedience to the command, *"all* prayer and supplication"! The context of this command refers to hand-to-hand combat with the enemy. In combat I don't just defend myself. I defend others as well. Likewise in spiritual battle, I don't just pray for myself, I pray for others too. Something quite transformational occurs when in the midst of my own challenges and spiritual battles I turn my focus in prayer on someone else. Intercession for others can bring victory to our own lives. Let's look at a scriptural example.

The Lord gave Satan access to Job for a divine reason: "And the Lord said to Satan, 'Behold, all that he has is in your power; only do not lay a hand on his person.' So Satan went out from the presence of the Lord" *(Job 1:12).*

Job's wife concluded judgment had fallen on her husband and said to him, "...'Do you still hold fast to your integrity? Curse God and die!" *(Job 2:9).*

To add to his problems, the Lord allowed his three friends Eliphaz, Bildad, and Zophar to become his worst critics. This trio troubled Job throughout his satanically-designed trials with their man-made ideas of why God was allowing these cataclysmic problems.

- "In all this Job did not sin nor charge God with wrong" *(Job 1:22)*.

- "And the Lord restored Job's losses when he prayed for his friends. Indeed the Lord gave Job twice as much as he had before" *(Job 42:10)*.

The Lord wanted Job, in the midst of his worst warfare nightmare, to pray for his friends. Intercession! God was saying, Job, take your eyes off yourself and all your troubles. I want you to pray for your critics and detractors.

That type of prayer is impossible unless one is filled with the Holy Spirit.

Quite often demons work to bring us into the boxing ring of great problems and trials through devious people. We are commanded to pray for everyone involved in our warfare, even those who are agents in our pain. Just like in Job's case, not everyone will understand the reasons why you are enduring demonic attack. Fellow believers will come to all kinds of conclusions, many of which won't be accurate. Don't react negatively. Keep your eyes fixed on Jesus and keep your heart filled with thanksgiving, intercession for others, and the love of Christ.

I have found whenever the Lord allows a believer to suffer, He generally builds an audience that can watch. As we live through our suffering, pain, trial, temptation, and spiritual conflict, we can preach the greatest sermon with the way we conduct ourselves if we keep our heart and attitude right. We are to follow Jesus' example. "Looking unto Jesus, the author and finisher of our faith, who for the joy that was set before Him endured the cross, despising the shame, and has sat down at the right hand of the throne of God" *(Hebrews 12:2)*.

3. "Praying always with all prayer and supplication

in the Spirit" *(Ephesians 6:18c):* The biblical formula is for us to pray to the Father, through the Son, in the Spirit.

In the Old Testament Tabernacle, on a small, golden altar before the veil the priest burned incense (see Exodus 30:1-10; Luke 1:1-11). Incense is a picture of prayer. It had to be mixed according to God's plan, and could not be counterfeited by man.

The fire on the altar is a picture of the Holy Spirit. He takes our prayers and "ignites" them according to the will of God for the protection of the believer: "Likewise, the Spirit also helps in our weaknesses. For we do not know what we should pray for as we ought, but the Spirit Himself makes intercession for us with groanings which cannot be uttered. Now He who searches the heart knows what the mind of the Spirit is, because He makes intercession for the saints according to the will of God" *(Romans 8:26-27).*

It is possible to pray fervently in the flesh and never get through to God. It is also possible to pray quietly in the Spirit and see God's hand do great things. You must pray in the Spirit when you face intense spiritual warfare.

In the early days of my faith I read a powerful book about Christians whom the Lord had used in mighty ways. Each one of these Christians had had a decisive moment when they were filled with the Holy Spirit.

J. Hudson Taylor, the mighty missionary to China whose life influenced more than 1,000 men and women to share Christ in the Far East, referred to this spiritual empowerment as *The Exchanged Life.* If you try to work for God without the fullness of the Holy Spirit, you will burn out. Conversely, when you are filled with the Spirit and praying in the power of the Spirit, the worst demonic attack will only make you stronger and more useful in the Lord's hands.

4. "Praying always with all prayer and supplication in the Spirit, being watchful to this end with all

perseverance" *(Ephesians 6:18d):* "Watchful" means "keeping on alert."

When Nehemiah was rebuilding the walls of Jerusalem the enemy tried to stop the work through Nehemiah's demonically-inspired detractors—Sanballat, Tobiah and Geshem (see Nehemiah 6:1-19), who taunted him (God's man) and tried several strategies to stop the work of God.

Every time you are making progress in God's Word, the enemy will send demons along who will try to stop you, slow you down, hinder you, or malign you and the work. Expect this, and keep on high alert. Get your spiritual binoculars out and stay on point! The word "perseverance" simply means "to stick to it and not quit."

- "Rejoicing in hope, patient in tribulation" *(Romans 12:12).*

- "But we will give ourselves continually to prayer and to the ministry of the Word" *(Acts 6:4).*

Most of us quit praying just before God gives us victory. Keep praying till the Holy Spirit stops prompting you to pray, or the Father gives you His answer!

I find it quite fascinating that Paul adds the thought of perseverance. Yes, only the Lord delivers, but we must do our part: hang in there! Let your "scars" become your "spiritual stars." Allow the Lord to turn your disappointments into His dynamic, spiritual appointments.

Fruitful believers are built in the furnace of affliction and difficulty.

STEPS TO SPIRITUAL CONQUEST

- "Therefore submit to God. Resist the devil and he will flee from you. Draw near to God and he will draw near to you. Cleanse your hands, you sinners; and purify your hearts, you double-minded. Humble yourselves in the sight of the Lord, and He will lift you up" *(James 4:7,8,10).*

- "Nor give place to the devil" *(Ephesians 4:27).*

"Place" is translated from the word *topos*, meaning "any portion of space marked off from the surrounding territory." I like to think of *topos* as a space separated from space around it —like a drawer in a chest of drawers. For example, my tee-shirts are in a certain drawer separated from other clothing.

Wuest renders the above verse, "And stop *giving an occasion for acting (opportunity)* to the devil."[104] Here the word *topos* is used in the sense of "opportunity, power, and an occasion for acting."

For example, the occult provides an opportunity for demons to gain entrance in your life through a variety of means—the Ouija board, horoscope, séances, dark video games, TV, and movies. This is nothing new. It was happening during the time that Paul, under the inspiration of the Holy Spirit, penned Ephesians chapter six.

In Paul's day Ephesus was a first-century occult centre. During the city's heyday at the time of Paul, 127 60-foot ionic columns supported the Temple of Diana. The Temple of Diana covered an area 130 by 60 yards. It was deemed one of the wonders of the world. The Ephesian Temple of Diana was four times larger than the Parthenon in Athens.

By the first century AD, Romans ruled Ephesus and had substituted their goddess Diana for the Greek Artemis who was the resident goddess when the temple was originally constructed in the 8th century BC. The substitution of Diana appears to have provided the Ephesian silversmiths with a lucrative business as they peddled miniature statues of the temple. Their profit margin dropped substantially when the Apostle Paul came to the city and preached Christ in substitution for idolatry.

The temple represented a very diabolical and dark religion. It served as a banking and religious centre. Nearly 1,000 female priests, or cult prostitutes, worked from that occult centre and sold Diana's religion through consensual sex to willing Ephesian customers. Also, near the site of the Temple archaeologists have discovered human bones, suggesting the possibility of sacrifice.

Through Paul's preaching, former occult worshippers came to faith in Christ and joined the Ephesian Church. But, lest you feel removed from the dark practices of Paul's day, we too live in a spiritually dark age.

The paranormal has become normal entertainment today. I shun this type of entertainment because it gives Satan an "opportunity"—it opens our minds and hearts to demonic invasion and attack.

Let me remind you of Revelation 18:23 that reads, "For your merchants were the great men of the earth, for by your sorcery all the nations were deceived." The word "sorcery" is translated from the word *pharmakeia* which we transliterate as "pharmacy." It is the root of the English word "pharmaceuticals," or drugs.

I am convinced the abuse of drugs opens a person to demonic invasion and attack. Look no further than the tragic life of singing sensation, Whitney Houston. Whitney loved the Lord and had regular Bible studies while on the road and at home. She was raised in church and sang in a choir her mother directed. Very sadly, Whitney became addicted to pharmaceutical drugs, and spiritual and physical defeat ensued.

The same tragedy occurred to singer Michael Jackson. I will never forget the night I was flying in a private plane to Van Nuys, California with gospel icon Andraé Crouch. He told me that not long before his death Michael had called him and asked him who the Holy Spirit was. Jackson had been searching desperately, but was enslaved in a deep prescription drug addiction. Yes, there is a connection between drug abuse and demons.

It is possible for believers to open a "drawer," or area of life and give place to the devil. The abuse of drugs, alcohol, sexual permissiveness, pornography, over-indulgence in sports, fun, reckless living, behaviour that induces isolation, depression and any form of occult exploration will open "drawers" in your life very quickly.

HOW TO BREAK DEMONIC BONDAGE

To break demonic bondage in your life, take the following steps:

1. Step #1—Come under the authority of God and His Word in every area of your life.

The first step to spiritual victory is to "submit yourself to God" *(James 4:7)* in every attitude and area of your life. The Lord does not tolerate a bitter, complaining, negative spirit or attitude.

Remove any form of rebellion against God from your life. For example, if you have occult material in your possession, or where you reside, remove it immediately.

If a bitter spirit has been the catalyst for rebellion in your heart, fall on your knees and ask God to forgive you.

If you are engaged in relationships that are dishonouring to Jesus Christ, stop them.

Has someone treated you unfairly? Has someone near you become ill, or died leaving you questioning the kindness and love of God? Give all your unanswered questions to the Lord and say, Father, by faith I know you are working in ways I will never understand until I get to heaven.

- "Let this mind be in you which was also in Christ Jesus" *(Philippians 2:5).*

- "Do all things without complaining and disputing" *(Philippians 2:14).*

2. Step #2—Confess any sins of commission or omission. Claim the forgiveness of the Lord, and forgive yourself! We cannot have fellowship with the Lord and break demonic strongholds without completely abandoning sin and confessing it before Jesus Christ. Sin gives ground, or room for the devil.

Maybe you are saying, Jerry, something comes to mind, but I don't really know if it's sin in my life. It makes me feel spiritually powerless and defeated, but in my thinking it's a gray area.

My answer would be for you to practice what I try to do. In every area of your life simply ask, What would Jesus do? Follow His example. If he wouldn't do it, claim the forgiveness that Scripture promises:

- "If we confess our sins, He is faithful and just to forgive us our sins and to cleanse us from all unrighteousness" *(1 John 1:9).*

- "If we walk in the light as He is in light, we have fellowship with one another, and the blood of Jesus Christ His Son cleanses us from all sin" *(1 John 1:7).*

"He who sins is of the devil, for the devil has sinned from the beginning. For this purpose the Son of God was manifested that He might destroy the works of the devil. Whoever has been born of God does not sin, for His seed remains in him; and he cannot sin, because he has been born of God" *(1 John 3:8-9).*

The above is a very unfortunate translation in both the *Authorized* and *New King James* versions of the Bible that does not accurately reflect the tense of the original Greek text.

"Is born" is a perfect participle in Greek and indicates a past action with consequences *continuing* to the present. "He cannot sin" is present tense in Greek, and indicates the *habitual life* of sinning, not individual acts of sin. The text is not saying that a believer cannot commit sin, but that a true believer in Christ will not live a life of sinning habitually.

1 John 3:8 asserts, "The devil has sinned from the beginning." In Greek, the linear progressive present active indicative case is used. It renders the meaning: "the devil has been sinning from the beginning of his career." Sinning is therefore the devil's normal way of life, and those who habitually sin with no conscience and conviction of the Holy Spirit reveal that they are like him. Wuest is very precise in his explanation:

> 'Committeth' is poieō (ποιεω), in a present tense participle, 'He who is continually doing sin.' Smith suggests, 'He that makes sin his business or practice.' 'Of' is ek (ἐκ), 'out of,' used with the ablative case, gives us the ablative of source. He who continually does sin is out of the devil as a source.... Habitual actions again are an index of character, and here, of source.... 'Commit' is poieō (ποιεω) in the present tense which always speaks of continuous action unless the context limits it to punctiliar action, namely, the mere mention of the fact of the action, without the mentioning of details. The translation reads, 'Every one who has been born out of God, with the present result that he is a born-one (of God), does not habitually do sin.' 'His seed' refers to the principle of divine life in the believer. It is this principle of divine life that makes it impossible for a Christian to live habitually in sin, for the divine nature causes the child of God to hate sin and love righteousness, and gives him both the desire and the power to do God's will, as Paul says, 'God is the One who is constantly putting forth energy in you, giving you both the desire and power to do His good pleasure' (Philippians 2:13)."[105]

The devil tempts us to sin and then condemns us if we surrender to sin and temptation. I know a number of Christians who are sitting in the ruins of a good start because they tripped up along their spiritual journey. The Holy Spirit's power can help a believer resist and overcome any temptation, or sin that the devil uses to instigate disobedience to God. Don't let the devil trick you into thinking you can't gain spiritual victory. You can overcome any temptation, or sin through the power of Jesus in you.

"Therefore let him who thinks he stands take heed lest he fall. No temptation has overtaken you except such as is common to man; but God is faithful, who will not allow you to be tempted beyond what you are able, but with the temptation will also make the way of escape, that you may be able to bear it" *(1 Corinthians 10:12-13)*.

3. Step #3—Claim the power and blood of Jesus over your mind, body, heart, and life.

There is immense power in the blood and name of Jesus Christ. Positionally, as a Christian you are already seated with Jesus Christ in heaven. You are the King's kid! Heaven is your home. Your name is written in the Lamb's Book of Life in His blood.

Jesus defeated Satan and every demon in his army when He died on the cross and rose again the third day from the grave. The devil and his demons are not *going* to be defeated. They *already are* defeated! Christ's spiritual victory is your spiritual victory. Believe it! Claim it! Say to the devil, Satan, I resist you in the name and blood of Jesus Christ.

I have repeated that glorious statement hundreds of times in the years I have been a Christian. I don't converse with the devil or demons. I rebuke them in the authority of the Lord Jesus Christ. You can do the same!

Rebuke the lies demons are trying to load in your mind.

Rebuke the flesh that is weak toward sin.

Plead the blood of Jesus Christ that He shed on the cross to remove your sin for all eternity.

Quote the Word of God (your "spiritual sword") against every demon that comes against you.

Use the name of Jesus with boldness: "Therefore God also has highly exalted Him and given Him the name which is above every name, that at the name of Jesus every knee should bow, of those in heaven, and of those on earth, and of those under the earth, and that every tongue should confess that Jesus Christ is Lord, to the glory of God the Father" *(Philippians 2:9-11)*.

4. Step #4—Conform your life in spiritual distinction and obedience.

James promised, "Draw near to God and He will draw near to you" *(James 4:8a)*. You would be amazed how close you will feel to God if you spend one hour a day reading the Bible and praying. If you devote a mere 20 minutes a day to Scripture reading, you will complete the entire Bible in a year.

Decide today that you will read and study Scripture every day. Find your Bible, keep it close to you, and put God's Word into action. It will produce great power in your life.

As you spend time with God, keep a prayer journal. Record your prayer requests and the dates God sends you answers. Write out your prayers to the Lord. Sing and praise Him. As you do these things God will draw close to you and demons will flee.

Finally, find a good church. Look for a church where

- the pastor loves God's Word and disciplines himself to present substantive sermons so you can grow in your faith

- you can participate in a small group

- you can join a Bible study group

- you can worship freely.

Worship allows the believer to open his or her mind, heart, and emotions to the Lord. A great church committed to the authority of the Bible will have great worship that draws you into God's presence using songs that speak *to* Him instead of *about* Him.

Be faithful in your church attendance and watch the Lord bless, protect, and grow you in your faith.

Spiritual warfare is predictable, but even more sure is the power of Jesus Christ to lead you to spiritual victory!

DISCUSSION QUESTIONS

1. Reflect on your commitment to memorize Scripture. Share your experience with others in your group. What hindrances do you experience to memorization?

2. What three things did Scripture do in Jerry's life?

3. What is the difference between prayer in the flesh and prayer in the Spirit? Why is prayer in the Spirit effective? What three things did prayer do in Jerry's life?

4. Why did Martin Luther pray two to three hours a day? Reflect on the time you spend in prayer. Can you commit to one hour of prayer and Bible reading every day? Keep a journal and track your progress.

5. What four components of warfare prayer does Paul delineate in Ephesians 6:18?

6. Name some ways in which it is possible for a believer to open up areas of his life to demonic attack.

7. Are there areas or attitudes in your life that are not pleasing to God? What steps should you take to break demonic bondage in these areas of your life?

END NOTES

INTRODUCTION

1A Annette Lamothe-Ramos, "Beelzebub's Daughter: How Zeena Schreck Escaped The Church of Satan The Vice Guide To 'The Master,'" http://www.vice.com/en_ca/read/beelzebubs-daughter-0000175-v19n4 (accessed March 10, 2013). – 11

2A Email to the author from Corrine Public Rep., February 27, 2013, www.zeena.eu (accessed March 10, 2013). – 11

3A Bob Silver, "The Day Death Died," Into the Wardrobe – a C. S. Lewis web site, http://cslewis.drzeus.net/papers/easter.html (accessed March 10, 2013). – 15

4A Timothy L. Thomas (April 2003). "New Developments in Chinese Strategic Psychological Warfare," www.iwar.org.ul/psyops/resources/china/chincscpsyop.pdf (accessed March 10, 2013). – 16

CHAPTER 1

1) Charles R. Swindoll, Demonism: *How to Win Against the Devil*, Insight for Living, P. O. Box 269000, Plano, TX 75026. – 20

2) Michael Green, *I Believe in the Holy Spirit* (Grand Rapids: Wm. B. Eerdmans Publishing, 2004), 278. – 22

3) John MacArthur, *Our Sufficiency in Christ* (United States: Crossway Books, 1998), 248. – 23

4) John R. Rice, *The Charismatic Movement* (United States: Sword of the Lord Publishers, 1978 – 24

5) Theodore Epp, *Back to the Bible*, P. O. Box 82808, Lincoln, NE 68501. – 25

6) The International Standard Bible Encyclopedia, http://www.internationalstandardbible.com/D/demon-demoniac-demonology.html (accessed February 4, 2013). – 26

7) p. 48. – 26

CHAPTER 2

8) Merrill F. Unger, *Biblical Demonology* (Grand Rapids: Kregel Publications, 1994), vii – 34

9) G.H. Pember, *Earth's Earliest Ages* (United States: Kregel Publications, 1975), 59. – 38

10) Merrill F. Unger, *Biblical Demonology* (Grand Rapids: Kregel Publications, 1994), 43. – 38

11) Clarence Larkin, *Rightly Dividing the Word of Truth*, (United States: Kessinger Publications, 2003), 94. – 38

12) Merrill F. Unger, *Biblical Demonology* (Grand Rapids: Kregel Publications, 1994), 43. – 39

13) Merrill F. Unger, *Biblical Demonology* (Grand Rapids: Kregel Publications, 1994), 27. – 39

14) Bob Deffinbaugh, "The Deliverance the Demoniac or 'Unholy Fear' (Luke 8:26-39)", http://bible.org/seriespage/ deliverance-demoniac-or-unholy-fear-luke-826-39 (accessed January 29, 2013). – 40

15) *The Nelson Study Bible* (Nashville: Thomas Nelson) – 40,41 http://www.thomasnelson.com/bibles/study-bibles.html (accessed February 1, 2013). – 41

16) William Barclay, *The Letter of James and Peter* (Philadelphia: Westminster John Knox Press, 2003), 32. – 41

17) William Barclay, *The Letter of James and Peter* (Philadelphia: Westminster John Knox Press, 2003), 33. – 41

18) John MacArthur, *1 & 2 Peter* (Nashville: Thomas Nelson, 2006), 27. – 42

19) Merrill F. Unger, *Biblical Demonology* (Grand Rapids: Kregel Publications, 1994), 62. – 43

20) *The Nelson Study Bible* (Nashville: Thomas Nelson) http:// www.thomasnelson.com/bibles/study-bibles.html (accessed February 1, 2013). – 44

CHAPTER 3

21) Charles H. Spurgeon, "Satanic Hindrances," http://www.spurgeongems.org/vols10-12/chs657.pdf (accessed January 17, 2013). – 50

22) Jake Arnott, "Aleister Crowley's lives: The Satanist and spy has inspired memorable characters," www.telegraph.co.uk/culture/books/5407318/Aleister-Crowleys-lives.html (accessed March 25, 2013).– 53

CHAPTER 4

23) John Nevius, *Demon Possession and Allied Themes* (Charleston: Nabu Press, 2011), 46. – 62

24) M. Scott Peck, *People of the Lie: The Hope for Healing Human Evil* (New York, Touchstone, 1998), 67. – 62

25) Merrill F. Unger, *Biblical Demonology* (Grand Rapids: Kregel Publications, 1994), 73. – 66

26) Kurt E. Koch, *Demonology Past and Present* (Grand Rapids: Kregel Publications, 2000), 83. – 66

27) Lechler, Alfred, "Symptoms of Demonization," www.lib.znate.ru?docs/index-238999.html?page=8 (accessed March 25, 2013).– 67

28) Merrill F. Unger, *Biblical Demonology* (Grand Rapids: Kregel Publications, 1994), 92. – 67

29) Merrill F. Unger, *Biblical Demonology* (Grand Rapids: Kregel Publications, 1994), 101. – 68

30) Merrill F. Unger, *Biblical Demonology* (Grand Rapids: Kregel Publications, 1994), 103. – 70

31) Merrill F. Unger, What Demons Can Do To Saints (Chicago: Moody Press, 1991), 5. – 71

32) Merrill F. Unger – 72

33) Hal Lindsey, *Satan is Alive and Well on Planet Earth* (Grand Rapids: Zondervan, 1972), 104. – 73

34) John MacArthur, *Colossians Philemon* (Nashville: Thomas

Nelson, 2007), 64. – 75

35) John MacArthur, *1 Peter* (Chicago: Moody Publishers, 2004), 56. – 76

CHAPTER 5

36) R. C. H. Lenski, *The Interpretation of 1 Corinthians* (Minneapolis: Augsburg Fortress Publishers, 2008), 278. – 81

37) Warren Wiersbe, *1 Corinthians: Be Wise* (Colorado Springs: Chariot Victor Publishers, 1984), 76. – 81

38) Charles Hodge, *1 Corinthians* (Wheaton: Crossway, 1995), 45. – 82

39) Robert Gromacki, *Called to Be Saints: 1 Corinthians* (The Woodlands: Kress Christian Publications, 2001), 81. – 83

40) Marvin Vincent, *Word Studies in the New Testament* (Grand Rapids: Eerdmans, 1976), 401. – 84

CHAPTER 6

41) J. Vernon McGee, *Ephesians* (Nashville: Thomas Nelson Publishers, 1995), 31. – 95

42) William Barclay, *The Gospel of Mark* (Philadelphia: Westminster John Knox Press, 2001), 98. – 95

43) Hank Hanegraaff, *Christianity in Crisis* (Eugene: Harvest House, 1993), 44. – 97

44) Charles Spurgeon, Faith, http://www.spurgeon.org/sermons/0107.htm (accessed January 28, 2013). – 100

45) Charles F. Pfeiffer, Editor, *The Wycliffe Bible Commentary* (Chicago: Moody, 1962), 459. – 103

46) William Barclay, *The Gospel of John* (Philadelphia: Westminster John Knox Press, 2001), 176. – 103

47) *The Nelson Study Bible* (Nashville: Thomas Nelson) http://www.thomasnelson.com/bibles/study-bibles.html (accessed February 10, 2013). – 104

48) Oswald Chambers, *My Utmost For His Highest* (Grand

Rapids: Discovery House, 1992), 278. – 104

CHAPTER 7

49) J. Vernon McGee, *Thru the Bible, Volume 5: 1 Corinthians – Revelation* (Nashville: Thomas Nelson, 1994), 93. – 111

50) John MacArthur, *1 Corinthians* (Nashville: Thomas Nelson, 2006), 86. – 111

51) J. Vernon McGee, *Thru the Bible, Volume 5: 1 Corinthians – Revelation* (Nashville: Thomas Nelson, 1994), 94. – 113

52) John MacArthur, *1 Corinthians* (Nashville: Thomas Nelson, 2006), 88. – 113

53) Charles Hodge, *1 Corinthians* (Wheaton: Crossway, 1995), 61. – 114

CHAPTER 8

54) D. L. Moody, http://godismylife.wordpress.com/page/2/ (accessed February 3, 2013). – 132

55) Harold J. Ockenga, Faithful in Christ Jesus (London: Fleming H. Revell Company, MCMXLVIII), p. 298. – 133

56) John Phillips, *Exploring Ephesians & Philippians: An Expository Commentary* (Grand Rapids, MI: Kregel Publications, 1993), pp. 189-190. – 134

CHAPTER 9

57) Martin Lloyd Jones, *The Christian Soldier* (Grand Rapids, MI: Baker Books, 1977), 182. – 146

58) John Stott, *The Message of Ephesians* (Downers Grove: IVP Academic, 1996), 58. – 147

59) Easton, M. G. (1996). *Easton's Bible Dictionary*. Oak Harbor, WA: Logos Research Systems, Inc. – 148

60) John MacArthur, *The MacArthur New Testament Commentary Ephesians* (Chicago: Moody Press, 1986), 351. – 149

61) Ernest Best, *The International Critical Commentary of Ephesians* (London: T & T Clark, 1998), 598. – 149

62) John MacArthur, *The MacArthur New Testament Commentary Ephesians* (Chicago: Moody Press, 1986), 353. – 156

63) John Phillips, *Exploring Ephesians & Philippians* (Grand Rapids: Kregel, 1993), 195. – 157

64) Max Anders, *Holman New Testament Commentary on Ephesians* (Nashville: Broadman & Holman, 1999), 191. – 159

CHAPTER 10

65) Charles Colson, *The Body* (Nashville: Word, 1992), 121. – 164

66) Warren Wiersbe, *Wycliffe Handbook of Preaching and Preachers* (Chicago: Moody Press, 1984), 220. – 164

67) C. H. Spurgeon, *Exploring the Mind & Heart of the Prince of Preachers* (Oswego, IL: Fox River Press, 2005), 403. – 165

68) C. H. Spurgeon, *Exploring the Mind & Heart of the Prince of Preachers* (Oswego, IL: Fox River Press, 2005), 404. – 166

69) John Phillips, *Exploring Ephesians & Philippians: And Expository Commentary* (Grand Rapids: Kregel, 1995), 196. – 170

70) Harold J. Ockenga, *Faithful in Christ Jesus* (New York: Fleming H. Revell Company, MCMXLVIII), 240. – 170

71) D. Martyn Lloyd-Jones, *The Christian Soldier: An Exposition of Ephesians 6:10-20* (Grand Rapids: Baker Book House, 1977), 300. –174

72) D. Martyn Lloyd-Jones, *The Christian Soldier: An Exposition of Ephesians 6:10-20* (Grand Rapids: Baker Book House, 1997), 301. — 175

73) D. Martyn Lloyd-Jones, *The Christian Soldier: An Exposition of Ephesians 6:10-20* (Grand Rapids: Baker Book House, 1977), 301. – 178

74) John Phillips, *Exploring Ephesians & Philippians: An Expository Commentary* (Grand Rapids: Kregel, 1995), 197. – 179

75) C. H. Spurgeon, *Exploring the Mind & Heart of the Prince of Preachers* (Oswego: Fox River Press, 2005), 404. – 181

CHAPTER 11

76) Barna Research Online, "Discipleship Insights Revealed in Book by George Barna," www.barna.org/cgi-bin/ PagePressRelease.asp?PressReleaseID=76&Reference=E&Ke y=bible%20knowledgeNovember28,2000 (accessed March 3, 2013). – 184

77) Gary M. Burge, "The Greatest Story Never Read: Recovering Biblical Literacy in the Church," www. christianitytoday.com/ct/9t9/9t9045.html (accessed March 3, 2013). – 184

78) Ibid. – 185

79) George Lindbeck, *The Church's Mission to a Postmodern Culture, Postmodern Theology: Christian Faith in a Pluralist World* (San Francisco: Harper & Row Publishers, 1989), 45. – 185

80) David F. Wells, *No Place For Truth or Whatever Happened to Evangelical Theology?* (Grand Rapids: Eerdmans, 1993), 4. – 185

81) "Biblical Illiteracy Spreading Among Christians," http:// news.crosswalk.com/partner/Article_Display_Plage/0,,PTID 74088%7CCHID194343%7CCIID1138212 (accessed March 3, 2013). – 185

82) Richard Morgan, "The Scandal of Biblical Illiteracy," Christianity Today *(May 7, 1965)*, 17. – 186

83) George Barna and Mark Hatch, *Boiling Point: It Only Takes One Degree* (Ventura: Regal, 2001), 187. – 188

84) The Bible Literacy Project, http://www.bibleliteracy.org/ site/Case/index.htm (accessed February 27, 2013). – 188

85) Ibid. – 189

86) Stephen Prothero, *Religious Literacy: What Every American Needs to Know – and Doesn't* (San Francisco: HarperSanFrancisco, 2007), 59, 62. – 190

87) Wiersbe, W. W. (1996). *The Bible Exposition Commentary* (Eph 6:13). Wheaton, IL: Victor Books. – 190

88) Ibid, 65, 66. – 191

89) Ibid, 67. – 191

90) Ibid, 70. New England Primer, Noah Webster's Speller, McGuffey's Readers. – 191

91) Ibid, 80 – 192

92) Ibid, 84. – 192

93) Wuest, K. S. (1997). *Wuest's Word Studies from the Greek New Testament: For the English Reader* (Heb 13:5). Grand Rapids: Eerdmans. – 194

94) Vincent, M. R. (1887). *Word Studies in the New Testament* (Eph 6:16). New York: Charles Scribner's Sons. – 194,195

95) Liberty Bible Commentary (Nashville: Thomas Nelson Publishers, 1994), 2427. – 195

96) Wuest, K. S. (1997). *Wuest's Word Studies from the Greek New Testament: For the English Reader* (Eph 6:14). Grand Rapids: Eerdmans. – 195

97) Keener, C. S. (1993). *The IVP Bible Background Commentary: New Testament* (Eph 6:16). Downers Grove, IL: InterVarsity Press. – 195

98) Arthur G. Patzia, *New International Biblical Commentary: Ephesians, Philippians, Colossians, Philemon* (Peabody, Massachusetts: Hendrickson Publishers, 1990), 289. – 196

99) C. H. Spurgeon, *Exploring the Mind & Heart of the Prince of Preachers* (Oswego, IL: Fox River Press, 2005), 152-153. – 196

100) Heidi Glenn, Losing Our Religion: The Growth

of the 'Nones,' http://www.npr.org/blogs/thetwo-way/2013/01/14/169164840/losing-our-religion-the-growth-of-the-nones (accessed March 4, 2013). – 199

101) Religion, Children and the Rise of the 'Nones,' http://radioboston.wbur.org/2013/01/14/nones (accessed March 4, 2013). – 199

102) John Phillips, Exploring Ephesians & Philippians (Grand Rapids: Kregel, 1993), 195. – 203

CHAPTER 12

103) Wuest, K. S. (1997). *Wuest's Word Studies from the Greek New Testament: For the English Reader* (Eph 6:18). Grand Rapids: Eerdmans. – 208

104) Wuest, K. S. (1997). *Wuest's Word Studies from the Greek New Testament: For The English Reader* (Eph. 4:26-28). Grand Rapids: Eerdmans. – 215

105) Ibid., (1 John 3:8). – 219

FOR FURTHER READING

Biblical Demonology, by Merrill F. Unger,
(Grand Rapids: Kregel Publications, 1994)

The Body, by Charles Colson, (Nashville: Word, 1992)

Boiling Point: It Only Takes One Degree, by George Barna
and Mark Hatch, (Ventura: Regal, 2001)

Called to Be Saints: 1 Corinthians, by Robert Gromacki,
(The Woodlands: Kress Christian Publications, 2001)

The Charismatic Movement, by John R. Rice,
(United States: Sword of the Lord Publishers, 1978

Christianity in Crisis, by Hank Hanegraaff,
(Eugene: Harvest House, 1993)

The Christian Soldier, by Martin Lloyd Jones,
(Grand Rapids, MI: Baker Books, 1977)

*The Church's Mission to a Postmodern Culture, Postmodern
Theology: Christian Faith in a Pluralist World,* by George
Lindbeck, (San Francisco: Harper & Row Publishers, 1989)

Demonism: How to Win Against the Devil, by Charles R.
Swindoll, *Insight for Living,* P. O. Box 269000, Plano, TX
75026.

Demonology Past and Present, by Kurt E. Koch,
(Grand Rapids: Kregel Publications, 2000)

Demon Possession and Allied Themes, by John Nevius,
(Charleston: Nabu Press, 2011)

Earth's Earliest Ages, by G.H. Pember,
(United States: Kregel Publications, 1975)

Ephesians, by J. Vernon McGee,
(Nashville: Thomas Nelson Publishers, 1995)

Exploring Ephesians & Philippians, by John Phillips,
(Grand Rapids: Kregel, 1993)

Exploring the Mind & Heart of the Prince of Preachers,
C. H. Spurgeon, (Oswego, IL: Fox River Press, 2005)

Faithful in Christ Jesus, by Harold J. Ockenga,
(New York: Fleming H. Revell Company, MCMXLVIII)

The Gospel of John, by William Barclay,
(Philadelphia: Westminster John Knox Press, 2001)

The Gospel of Mark, by William Barclay,
(Philadelphia: Westminster John Knox Press, 2001)

I Believe in the Holy Spirit, by Michael Green,
(Grand Rapids: Wm. B. Eerdmans Publishing, 2004)

My Utmost For His Highest, by Oswald Chambers,
(Grand Rapids: Discovery House, 1992)

*No Place For Truth or Whatever Happened to Evangelical
Theology?* by David F. Wells, (Grand Rapids: Eerdmans, 1993)

Our Sufficiency in Christ, by John MacArthur,
(United States: Crossway Books, 1998)

People of the Lie: The Hope for Healing Human Evil,
by M. Scott Peck, (New York, Touchstone, 1998)

*Religious Literacy: What Every American Needs to
Know—and Doesn't,* by Stephen Prothero, (San Francisco:

HarperSanFrancisco, 2007)

Rightly Dividing the Word of Truth, by Clarence Larkin, (United States: Kessinger Publications, 2003)

Satan is Alive and Well on Planet Earth, by Hal Lindsey, (Grand Rapids: Zondervan, 1972)

What Demons Can Do To Saints, by Merrill F. Unger, (Chicago: Moody Press, 1991)

SCRIPTURE INDEX

CHAPTER 7

CHAPTER 8

TOPIC INDEX

CHAPTER 3

CHAPTER 5

CHAPTER 6

CHAPTER 7

CHAPTER 8

CHAPTER 10

CHAPTER 12

ABOUT THE AUTHOR

Jerry Johnston (Doctor of Ministry—Acadia University Divinity College, Wolfville, Nova Scotia) has captivated more than 4,000,000 youth on more than 2,500 public school campuses, addressing vital issues. He has held events in more than 1,200 churches of all denominations throughout the United States and Canada. More than 125,000 people have come to faith in Jesus Christ through his invitation. Jerry has authored 13 books and produced 12 videos that have been distributed to thousands of churches. He has presented 112 different popular teaching series comprised of over 900 expositional messages on video, many of which are available online.

While still in high school, Jerry's ministry career began as an Evangelist-at-Large for Youth for Christ, the same ministry that launched Billy Graham. Later, Jerry was awarded an Honorary Doctor of Divinity degree (1997).

Dr. Johnston has extensive media experience and has been interviewed on *Fox News' The O'Reilly Factor, Good Morning America, World News Tonight, Nightline; The Today Show,* CNN*'s Crossfire,* Deborah Norville Tonight, MSNBC's Scarborough Country, *Connected Coast to Coast with Ron Reagan, Focus on the Family, The 700 Club, 100 Huntley Street* in Canada, and many others.

Jerry's wife, Dr. Cristie Jo Johnston, is an effective teacher of God's Word who has broad appeal to both men and women. The Johnston's have three children: Danielle, married to Christian Newsome, senior pastor of The Journey Church, Lee's Summit, MO; Jeremiah Johnston, Ph.D., Lecturer in

Biblical Studies, Acadia Divinity College, married to Audrey; and Jenilee, married to Jeffrey Mullikin.

Jerry has served as an effective consultant to pastors and various ministries on media development, fundraising, and mentoring leaders.

To schedule Jerry to speak in your church, school, or area write or call:

In Canada:	In the United States:
Crossroads	Crossroads
Box 5100	P. O. Box 486
Burlington, ON	Niagara Falls, NY
L74 4M2	14302

905-332-6400, ext. 3307

 Jerry Johnston on Twitter:
@jerry_johnston

 Jerry Johnston on Facebook:
facebook.com/DrJerryJohnston

IF YOU ENJOYED *CHRISTIANS & DEMONS*, SHARE ITS MESSAGE WITH OTHERS ...

- Mention the book in a Facebook post, Twitter update, Pinterest pin, or blog post. Be sure to "Like Us" at **facebook.com/crossroads.ca**.

- Recommend this book to your small group, Bible study, book club or workplace, and consider using it as a multi-week curriculum.

- Tweet "I recommend reading *Christians & Demons.*"

- Go to **crossroads.ca** and order a quantity of *Christians & Demons* for your small group or Bible study so that people you know can be challenged, informed and encouraged through this message.

- Peruse our e**store** at **crossroads.ca/store** for quality resources for your faith journey. We have many resources such as Bibles, Bible studies, books on a variety of topics, CDs and DVDs. We also provide free shipping for orders over $100. For personal assistance in ordering, call **1-800-265-3100.**

- Watch video clips on this and other topics: **crossroads360.com**

- Sign up for the Crossroads eNewsletter: **crossroads.ca.**